Pages

Pages

NEW POEMS AND CUTTINGS

John Matthias

Swallow Press/Ohio University Press

Athens

Swallow Press/Ohio University Press, Athens, Ohio 45701
© 2000 John Matthias
Printed in the United States of America
All rights reserved. Published 2000

Swallow Press/Ohio University Press books are printed on acid-free paper ⊗ ™

05 04 03 02 01 00   5 4 3 2 1

Library of Congress Cataloging-in-Publication Data

Matthias, John, 1941–
    Pages : new poems and cuttings / John Matthias.
        p.   cm.
    ISBN 0-8040-1019-6 (cloth : alk. paper). — ISBN 0-8040-1020-X (paper : alk. paper)
    I. Title.
PS3563.A858P34 1999
811'.54—dc21   99-32582

Contents

Part II
Pages: *From a Book of Years*

Part III
Cuttings

Acknowledgments

Acknowledgment is due to the editors of the following journals which first pub-
lished some of the poems appearing in this book:

Salmagundi
PN Review
Parnassus
Another Chicago Magazine
Bellingham Review
The New Criterion
Samizdat
Private Arts
TriQuarterly
Partisan Review
Boston Review

Poems

A Shared Garden in May

White scrubbed picnic table
with a potted bright red flower

leaning toward the Spanish girl
who writes a letter.

She's in the garden
and she's got her window up

to hear the record or the tape
she's just put on. . . .

Hallelujah! Hallelujah sings
a choir from Barcelona

or from some such distant place.
We're in Saratoga, she and I.

Her letter's doubtless going to
some old friend overseas

or to her mother, say,
or her sister or an uncle even.

Everything's okay for the moment.
The choir sings *Hallelujah!*

the picnic table gleams,
the flower leans toward the girl

writing the letter, and I
who left the flower on the table

(I forgot to bring it in with
all the groceries)

sit here doubtfully in May
with cans and cabbages and look.

On Rereading a Friend's First Book

You are 4000 miles away &
This world did not invite us.
— ROBERT HASS

These poems discussed by all the critics now
as if they had been written by a poet
dead a hundred years—

How young we were!

I see my poet in parodic costume
mumming Marshal Ky
or maybe General Westmoreland
as all of us around the burning microphone
give the finger to the war
and Stanford's Hoover Institute.
Everything was art and politics and Eros.

Everything was Eros.

Why is there nostalgia for incendiary times?
Because some Helen's at
the center of the fire. That girl in the t-shirt
and the shorts who loves your voice,
who puts your words into her mouth, who
comes back to your room when all the speeches
have been made.

I knew her too. You wrote of longing
and desire as if they could undo
the malice of the times.
You burned at night like napalm.
Now those days
are like the pyracanthas in these poems,
and we like waxwings, drunk on them.

The world looks almost to have invited us.

Two in New York

I: Easter 1912

His name was Frédéric Sauser his name
was Blaise Cendrars his name was Nineteen Twelve
his name was Eiffel Tower.

Only later Sonia Delaunay and Trans-Siberian Prose,
later loss of a good right arm at the Marne.
His name that day it was Pâques might have been Ray—

Ray of Gourmont that Easter and everyone gone.
Nobody liturgy nobody nun nobody
anthem or song or prelate or incense or drum.

So *dic nobis quid vidisti*: nobody nobody there
when he woke and wrote down his name
in New York it was Fear. What could he do but go home?

II: Christmas 1929

And what could *he* do, Chien Andalou,
whose speech had the fire of flamenco guitar,
whose eyes were the gypsies of war.

Federico gracias gracias (loricated legionaries
looking like a Guardia Civil before its time,
the Harlem jazzmen blowing bagels from the bells

of saxophone and horn: *Christus natus est*)—
Feed the poor on *cante jondo*, give the weary rest.
But what could he do, Chien Andalou,

Poeta en Nueva York? Shiva looked like Ramadan.
And yet the girls were rain. He'd ransom every
singing boy he'd die for, and he'd die for it in Spain.

Easter 1912 and Christmas 1929: Blaise Cendrars and Garcia Lorca in New York (a second take)

What lengths what loops. In 1912 and
good enough. In 1929.
At Easter first, at Pâques. And then a good
right hand and arm blown off
the shoulder at the Battle of the Marne.
And after 1930, the Falange.
But Easter first, but Christmas next again.
A calendar, a caliper.
And One:
who'd done a juggling act with Chaplin
in the London circus once.
One: who'd hear
a violin in limousine, a xylophone in linotype.
Who'd call out *Negro Negro* to the King
of Harlem looking for the Gypsy Jesus Christ.
In 1912, in 1929.
Caruso sang Puccini & the widows in black
carried his cross through the Bronx.
Whose Red Christ or whose Black Sun split
apart like a coal? Did somebody say
Je connais . . . Je descends
à grands pas vers le bas de la ville?
Did somebody answer
with wheel and leather and hammer and oil?
Ninguno quería ser . . .
Ninguno amaba las hojas, la lengua azul.
First Cendrars in 1912. And Lorca next.
One: These three:
Chalice and orchid and book. All the Christs
all the heists in museums. Nobody
there to hear bells, nobody anthem and song,
nobody liturgy, nobody nun, nobody
prelate or drum.
So *dic nobis quid vidisti* nobody nobody
there: Encores encipher at dawn.
Ten: What tense? Who'd tell

what tensions tore the whorish times.
They're all at nines who once were six & seven.
War and crash and war once more
within the loops upon the lengths & tongs.
The Russians all wore sarafans the cats
all wore kokoshniks.
Only Andalusians barked like the dogs.
Where bankrupts dealt in a contraband Duende
how could you dwell in the Blancos del Oro
Kingdom come where nobody came?
One: who dressed himself like a bride.
One: *que se viste de novia*.
One: who came back all alone to his room
whose bed was cold as a tomb
who had heard a hundred thousand women sing,
a hundred thousand cellos:
Cent milles femmes, cent milles violoncelles.
One: These Two.
Blaise Cendrars and Chien Andalou
with flamenco guitar.
In 1912 good enough in 1929.
Before the Marne before the carnage in Spain.
At Easter first, but Christmas next again.
Chalice and orchid and book.
Length and loop, anthem and gongs,
limousine xylophone linotype library songs.

Two after Branko Miljković

I - Inventory of a Poem

Here before all darkness
is the darkness which illuminates

After that the freedom of the beast to be a beast
And freedom of the snail to be a snail

Before all else the freedom of the birds to lose their way in space

After that the imagination of love
After that prestige of day over the career of fire

A stone grows heavier if it doesn't change

After that the first employment of useless things
The famous cat under the skin of the sphinx

An animal without a Sunday

II - The Past of Fire

It teaches the stars to be scornful
It cohabits with time

It sleeps in its own darkness out of severity
Mixing its ash with the freshness of day

It glows: its emptiness glows
Its infirmity enlightens all our roads

The sun is the name of its tyranny
The human heart hides in its betrayals

It acknowledges the north
In old age it blesses the terrible cold

The bird creating itself from its wantonness
Reads the ice from its mind

And the polluted fire in the head, the earlier word
Teaches cruelty to a future dawn

After the Serbian, with Vladeta Vučković

Three from Sonnevi's *Small Chimes*

I

Even the faces that love
carry the heart of treason   and it won't
cost you a thing   We place
the face's ass on top of somebody else

Every sleeping face in
the world   The brittle girl
whose skin was made to tremble,
twitch at every word   And

the coarseness of my face next to hers
My sleep's heart was beating her
sleep's heart   She may already

have forgotten me, as one forgets
a dream   I have not forgotten
her   She was no dream

II

And the language will arrive at last
We do not know what's first
or what is last   The concepts will
define each other   The re-

alities define themselves   We
have named each other then   What is
your name?   I have already forgotten,
lost it   The permutations were

too many   We have been entangled for too
long   Bone of each other's bone
Word of each other's word   Now

we can't be disentangled, can't
be parted ever or at all?   No—
Even now together we stand up

III

Young starlings are moving now
in the grass, green so far, before
the flight   The blue tit beats on the pane
An airplane is heard in space

When death arrives it will arrive
in silence, later with an incredible roar
in burnt out ears   An incredible
light, in blinded eyes

What help to us the darkness of an image
We have nowhere to go   We are
no longer even like the children

or the birds   Our souls whirl
in violent flight   The vortex of our language
in the greater vortex; through its eye—

After the Swedish of Göran Sonnevi
with Göran Printz-Pahlson

After Mnemosyne

If I tell her,
somewhere after the first game
came the caesura pause
bruise
and I am searching where

then:
from linden tree to music
to bicycle
and sand
to little laughs   cries under the leaves

& where?
searching out the place where images
can stay alone:
carpet edge,
papers . . .

                 or seated for an instant in a vase
                 on the terrace on all fours
                 mouth crammed with pins

the c
bruise
ah!
already here
or there

        (. . .)

After the French of Jacqueline Risset
with Catherine Perry

Two in Harar

I: Sir Richard Burton, 1854

He learned Somali from the soft and plaintive voice
of Kadima who allowed him to remove the leather lace
stitching up her labia and put two fingers in.

This was anthropology, linguistics. Topology and trade
would come in turn. Calling himself Haji Mirza Abdullah,
he wore a silken girdle with a dirk & chewed on khat

he found sufficiently priapic that in time he'd force his
member through infibulations of the local girls
without unlacing first. Now he rose and went to work.

He'd play the Amir off against al-Haji Sharmakay
on matters touching eunuchs and the slaves.
He'd demonstrate Koranic scholarship, say *Allahu Akhbar*.

He'd mesmerize them with his tales from the *Nights*.
His exegesis of *The Sura* dazzled all the mullahs
and he wisely took a local *abban* from among the Isas.

By the southwest coast near Zayla he turned inland,
riding on a donkey with a shotgun on his knee.
Everything that was not stone was sand. Everything that

was not sun was dust and wind. His bodyguards were
Long Gulad, The Hammal, End of Time.
They sang him Belwos, fed him holcus for his colic,

millet beer and boiled barks. If the nomads took him
he would learn phallotomy, his penis gone
for scholarship among the wives in someone's tent.

Bedu lurked about his camp and hurled stones.
They called him Old Woman, Chief of Zayla, Painted Man.
They called him Turk & Priest & Pilgrim—Merchant,

Banyan, and Calamity Sent Down from God.
He gave up his disguise and forged a letter from the
Aden consul introducing him as an ambassador

and dressed up in his captain's uniform with
epaulets and sword. He marched until he saw the walls
no white man ever breached, the gate he thought

he'd walk through chanting poems. Back in Zayla
they proclaimed him dead. Back in London
Karl Marx & Tennyson sat down to read his Mecca Haj.

The Amir asked him if he'd come to buy Harar.

II: Arthur Rimbaud, 1886–1888

And was Harar for Sale? And were *Le Voyant*'s visions
null and void? *Solde.* He'd left behind what time
nor science had acknowledged, drowned his book of magic

and returned to earth. And one must enter splendid cities
absolutely modern after all. Among the packs
of one-eyed mangy dogs. And with a taste for soil & stone.

His I was other and another still. His ear once made
him brass and like a bugle he had blown.
A scent of wood, he'd found himself a broken violin.

He did not think he knew and did not want to know
how he'd been thought into his poems.
He colored vowels no more and all of them went black.

He'd be a gun-butt now if he were wood;
if he were steel, a rail laid down in Africa for desert trains.
He studied business, engineering, crafts.

He'd sold unknown harmonic intervals for
proper calculation and would traffic
in the hides and coffee-beans and ivories of Somalia

living by the Raouf Pasha palace earning two percent
commission from Pierre Bardey on trade.
And when the Mahdi rose and Dervishes advanced

through Abyssinia, he mocked Kartoum's illuminated
English Gordon, rich Egyptians & the Turks,
and took a caravan of armaments on inland from Tajoura

and was ruined. He came back to Harar and tried to run
the trading station while in Paris decadents
proclaimed a system based entirely on his Sonnet of the Vowels.

Black A, white E, red I, blue O, green U.
Was he back where he belonged? This wasn't what Parnassians
had in mind. They might proclaim King Menelek

himself a symbolist if he became Negasti & Hararis were
his businessmen of Empire up and down their narrow streets.
There was no Amir left in town, no Wazir.

Sultan Ahmad bin Sultan Abibakr had asked Captain Burton
if he'd come to buy Harar. The poet advertised the sale
of priceless bodies, *hors de toute race, hors de tout monde*.

Travelers would not render their commission for a while.

Six or So in Petersburg

They go out to the theatre. It's Lermontov, his Masquerade.
Shostakovich might have made an opera of it
if they hadn't executed Meyerhold. But that comes later on.
Tonight it's Meyerhold's production, it is Petersburg,
it is no ordinary evening in October. Everybody's there.

Everybody who is anyone is there. Anna Andreyevna
only managed tickets for the dress rehearsal; she isn't
anybody who is anyone just yet. The beautiful Gorenka.
When she bites her tongue she tastes her Tartar blood.
She leaves a dress shop on the afternoon it all begins.

It all begins like theatre, like Masquerade, like Lermontov.
It all begins like Meyerhold. Perhaps those mummers
mime it all, perhaps the bodies lying in the street are only
doused with buckets of red paint. The painters all come too.
The painters and the dancers and the violinists mime.

All the dead men get back up to much applause.
All the dead men lie there in the streets. Either way
the beautiful Gorenka tastes her Tartar blood & speaks.
She makes a music of this Meyerhold, this Masquerade.
The lovesick Gumilyov tells her he is dead, a suicide.

Gumilyov is not dead, he only mimes. He's shot, of course,
but that comes later on. He is in Paris, not in Petersburg.
It's Knyazev who has killed himself for love. Who will die
for Vladimir Ulyanov? Everyone who goes to Masquerade.
Gorenka has become Akhmatova. She'll write it down.

They write down everything you say. The ones who ask
you where you live, who ask your name, who ask you
why you're playing in this Masquerade. Gumilyov rides his
wayward tram back home. He cannot tell the severed heads
from cabbages with heads so cheap on sale in every shop.

They come out of the theatre and stare at all the fires.
Petersburg is burning down. It is revised, with major cuts

provided by the censors. That is, the novel by Bely.
That is, his *Petersberg*. Nikolai Apollonovich stands before
his mirror as a blood-red domino in an assassin's mask:

His hand upon a bust of Kant. The mummers in the poem
by Anna Andreyevna mime another age on the Fontanka.
She conjures there a guest come from the future bringing doom
instead of flowers; she writes upon the writings of the dead.
There's Mandelstam; there's Meyerhold; there's Blok.

On the obverse, Pushkin's whispering *Your future is your past;
Drink the waters of Lethe*. And in her other ear the Engineer
of Souls: *Then tell us who is who and who's alive and who
is dead; we'll melt your triple-bottomed black libretto down into
a hymn of state and gift you with a row of dots out of Onegin.*

. . .

Shostakovich plays a movement from his Seventh as the shells
explode outside his flat. He wraps himself in Gogol's overcoat
and waits for the evacuation to begin. The painters will come too.
Someone must be there to pour the blood. Beneath the window
Peter on his high bronze horse pursues the fleeing mad Evgeny.

Scherzo Trio: Three at the Villa Seurat

I - Henry

I say fuck fuck fuck fuck fuck
in all my books.
Women I call cunts and men
except for Larry all are assholes.

Eliot declares that I'm a genius
but refuses all my books at Faber.
Cancer, Capricorn, Black Spring,
you get them cheap from Obelisk.

Fuck fuck fuck fuck fuck.
You read it there in all my books:
that women all are cunts and men
except for Larry all are assholes.

II - Larry

I write heraldic prose and someone
hits upon Baroque in a review.
But I don't like Baroque; I like
bouzouki music, I like Corfu.

I'd screw Anaïs like the rest of them
if she would let me in. Why am I
the only one who doesn't get it?
I said to Henry when I met him,

You're the only one with fever'd
brain enough to see the only way
for art to go today
is straight on down the sewer!

III - Anaïs

I'm delicate, incestuous, incessant
and insane. I sleep with
all my shrinks and none of them at all
are like my famous father.

Henry's only good for once a week
but that's a great improvement on Artaud.
My diary is better than the books
by all these crooks: They will be mine forever

when all their pages have been pulped.
Fashion is as fickle as a feather.
I do say clever things. Call me from my nap
if Edmund Wilson ever rings.

The Key of C Does Not Know My Biography
(Stravinsky, 1937–1942)

In Sancellemoz they read the *Philokalia* while
in the rue St. Honoré his *moderato alla breve* coughed
not once for Nicodemus on Mount Athos or
Makarius of Corinth even if the resurrection were Docetic
and the tonic a familiar C.
It was the worst year of his life.
Tuberculosis drowned his daughter Mika and
his wife at Sancellemoz; he himself and then Milena
spat up blood; his mother died
and Wehrmacht panzers rumbled toward the Maginot.
He wrote in C. He wrote *Larghetto concertante*
in the sanatorium and though it was no *Sacre du Printemps*
the spring would have its rites: fists of earth
thrown in open graves at Saint Geneviève.
He wrote in C in C in C, was diatonic in extreme
and in the suite of dances the fugatos
the Italianate transparency of theme you'd never
guess he lit the candles every night in agony
beside the image of *La Vierge de perpétuel secours*.

Then Hollywood. Then the *allegretto* and the *largo*
and the Disney dinosaurs roaring to Stokowsky's *Sacre*
that frightened little children at the matinees.
Then war. Then holocaust. He wrote in C.
His one entirely boring work had saved his life
by counting repetitions like the telling of a rosary—
dominant and tonic, tonic and the dominant—
tonal bricks to build a house in which he'd pitch at last
a tall dodecaphonic tent and
call the Angel down for Abraham.
He said the key of C
did not know his biography.

That Music Is the Spur to All Licentiousness
(Janáček in love)

The little birds would flutter to
his Katya's grave his Kyrie in Glagolitic
sing out lustily a *Gaspodi pomiluj.*
Salva! (Gloria!)
                      But *non credo in Signeur Dieu by god*
whispered every violin he heard
some gypsy Dorian raised fourth cantabile his word consumed &
sounding out *nápěvky* Ka-mi-la. Half his age
and twice his muse she'd be his Katya his Kabanova
his lesson to Renard & Reineke
on how to chase a fox in old Moravia. *Bystrouška!*

Still those two quartets would feed on crazy
Tolstoy fed on *Kreutzer* weeping presto by the moonlit
porch at Yasnaya Polyana: Tender Lyovochka all
undone and fucking Sonia in the nave of his own *niet*
a Pozdnychev strung out in Prague *sul ponticello.*
That music is the spur to all licentiousness
the maestro doubts. His love unconsummated he embraces
only sound. And it dissolves.
And when the Angel asks him would he
make his peace with God the dying Janáček replies
but what is peace
and what is would
and what is god Janáčková.

Received by Angels Singing Like the Birds
(Messiaen, 1992)

Venite . . . inginocchiatevi &
Susanna's answered
by a Garden Warbler and a Kakapo.
Figaro! Strings, cymbal, wind machine, les ondes—
those bells bells from Assisi.
L'Ange Voyageur steps from Fra Angelico's *Annunciation*
with his wings unfurled, his feathers
quinticolored red & yellow, blue & green & mauve,
and sings: *Cantico della creature cantico*
glissando Gerygone percussion tuned a new
Noh-Caledonian: *What is your name?*
Ondeolivier avec offrandes pas oubliées.
And suddenly a dawn sky of Skylarks. Orioles
and Lyrebirds, suddenly antiphony
of Icterine and Thrush. Semitone descent from A
as demisemiquaver . . .then
arpeggio of cloud,
tremolo among the shining shaken leaves.

For Kym

The Flagellant *(i.m. Percy Grainger)*

Italian wouldn't do at all
to tell his band the way they ought to feel
when they played the score.

Bundle it & jogtrot through these bars, he'd say:
Lower notes of woggle well to the fore.
Easy goes but cling it, louden lots!

He'd have them lay on with a will.
He'd play the flageolet.
Some there were who'd find his ways flagitious.

2.

Melbourne in the mornings of
a mother's love:—His pregnant Rose would
gaze upon Apollo's alabaster

on her dresser, pray that he be gifted with
the sinlessness of song, and hang
the horsewhip by the empty music stand.

This son of sunlight might just winch it
short of woggle, jogtrot where he ought to cling,
bungle where the lauding rose at dawn.

3.

Carried by that praise well round the world,
Mother's "Bubbles," now her "Perks," yammered
in his made up lingo to the friends who'd listen

while he stood up naked on the lid of his piano
talking Maori Swedish German & Icelandic
all at once and lecturing the Frankfurt musicologists

on Kipling. His *Marching Song* would be performed
by whistling girls tramping through the open air
in broken strides at who/4 what/4 & in double Dutch.

4.

The *Shorter Music Dictionary* (Willi Apel, Harvard)
has no listing for *Brigg Fair*. There's no mention
there that in 1900 PG wrote a Sea Song which required

a band of winds to play at 7/35 and 9/17. Between
the *Frauenliebe* songs and *Freischütz, Der*
you won't learn anything about Free Music or the

Melanette machine or Grainger glides accomplished
by the PG System Kangaroo. *Lulu's* listed,
Lute and *Lur*, but not PG's *A Lot of Rot for Cello*.

5.

Anyhow, Brigg Fair. The brown wax cylinders revolved
to capture every bleat & twiddle of the lads from
Lincolnshire whose mix of Dorian Aeolian Ionian

scaled up and down the modes the way their fathers had
before the sons had left for towns and music hall.
He scored it with the jagged rhythms and the ornaments

intact. He scored it with the slides and hugged himself
with joy. He rose up in the morning with the lark
and beat himself until he bled. He broke all out in clover.

6.

And no one knew quite what *The Warriors* was.
Not Lady Elcho in her country house, the PM's mistress
and the friend of H. G. Wells; not all the Wedgwoods

or the Wedgwood-Benns; not John Singer Sargent
or his spiffy sitters or the Balfours in their motor car.
It didn't just sing *Willow Willow*, not just *Shepherd's Hey*.

Did it appeal or appall? The rich were not apprised.
While Stabat Mater nursed *le vice anglais,*
it wore out three conductors and an offstage band.

7.

If he could call himself a tone-wright & his music tonery,
he'd purge the spirochete that gnawed in Greek
and Latin at the mothertongue's profoundest roots.

He said he wasn't democratic but a-chance-for-all-y,
and he'd pound out all his tone-works
on keyed-hammer-strings. Blue-eyed English word-seeds

should replace all but the most un-do-with-outable
post-Hastings-French-begottens too. He'd oh stick-to-it-
ively drive himself to overset his thot-plan into deeds.

8.

Or go to Norway, visit Grieg. Introduce Duke Ellington
to Delius. He'd play the Green Man guising like
a geezer's dream of Morris-dancing tribes. He wore

a coat from which there dangled gewgaws & galoshes,
pencils, pens & manuscripts all tied on with
little bits of string: his only suitcase was a suite of songs.

His robin was to the greenwood gone, his Kammermusik
Strathspey in the hills. If he wasn't Grettir he'd be
Gershwin oh or Mowgli in a decorated plagal & in G.

9.

But how did one make sounds that were the sea?
In what key was a cloud? Did winds blow sharp or flat?
And when his lovers beat him with the whips

how was he to score his mother's lips?
Must he orchestrate an algolagnia for algophobes?
He'd grow all logarithmical

at loggerheads with logos on the Loften Isles.
Blue-eyed English queried him—asked the why-grounds
for the hand-claps in the puzzle-wifty towns.

Master Class

Well, then, one more time.

Auf dem Flusse . . . where you
failed to emphasize the consonants enough
and your crescendo did not swell.
Der du so lustig rauschtest . . .
Liegst kalt. It's icy, understand?
What does a heartbeat sound like under ice?
Like this like this.
Let yourself be overcome by grief.

You can't? All right. Then let yourself
be overcome by joy.
Touch her and embrace her
as you did one summer on that river bank.
Unlace her bodice then. Your hand.
Right here. Heart, your heart
must break must break
because you know that she will die.

You are so young. You think these are clichés.
Your heart has never broken,
but it will. When I was young Isolde
Tristan died for me. I died for him.
You think this life is only song.
Begin again: Perhaps you favor French?
I am so old so old
and yet I do remember every touch.

So touch me. Here. Begin again, in French.
Shall you become my Pierrot Lunaire?
I'll sing for you from Berlioz:
Ma belle amie est morte.
You've never heard, I guess, of Gautier.
But if you care you'll die for me:
you'll die you'll die.
Here is the poison and the glass.

I am the mistress here, the maestro too.
This is my master class.
When you come, you'll sing it as I say.
You'll rhyme your *do*
with dildoe if I like.
You'll sing it sweetly while I play.
Der du so lustig rauschtest . . .
You'll sing it for me every day.

Diminished Third

I - Expectation

The woman clad in white, large red roses
shedding petals from her dress, expects
the unexpected, wanders through a moonlit woods
where, God knows, anyone might stumble
on their lover's corpse . . .
                            Even Schoenberg
in Vienna in *Erwartung*, improvising
ostinatos, overriding bars, or Hohenzollern Isoldes
spiking Bismarck helmets at the stars—

Even Moses, who could only speak, exclaiming
Ich will singen,
counting on his finger tips the laws.

II - Doctor Faust

Boxed by Thomas Mann into a magic square
with megrims, paedophiles and fictive sounds,
A.S. rages over stolen property, the rape and insult
perpetrated by this syphilitic Leverkühn who writes

a serialism no one ever heard. And yet he'd said himself
that music was a word, that language was a kind
of music too: Had in fact some rowdy losal out of hell
so pricked his blood with sophistries that nosy

novelists could smell the sulphur in his permutations?
Did *Volk* and *Führer* grow dodecaphonic in his
retrogrades, inversions; Hetaera Esmaralda somehow

ciphered in the h-e-a-e flat of it? *Sator Arepo*
tenet opera rotas. The opera would circle, right enough.
And the sower would sue for his tenet. In tenebrae.

III - The Golden Calf

Aron, was hast du getan

This Sprechstimme! This old dogmatic honky rapper
here before his time among the Angels.
He'd lecture all the Jews as all the Jews go down
all over Europe. He's safe and sound. His friend
is Mr. Gershwin and he beats the younger man
at tennis, ping pong, chess. He cannot win a Guggenheim,
cannot get performed.

Around him nothing but the idols
and the kitsch and the clichés. He's heard that in this
land of plenty no one gets a second act;
he cannot score a third and that's a fact.
Still the old Dodecaphon speaks while Aaron sings:
Ich will singen dinga dinga ding!
Anyone might stumble on a lover's corpse.

Is he Moses, Aaron, or their contradiction burning
in his brain like Leverkühn's disease?
Darf das Leid, mein Mund, dieses Bild machen?
Gershwin whistles happily: *I got plenty o' nuttin.*
Schoenberg spricht like eine glückliche hand:
Das Grenzenlose! Boundlessness!
Constellation upon constellation whirls.
Harmonielehre multiplies
by twelves through some 2000 bars and dies
with Volk and Führer.
So if the end, as Schnabel says, will justify the means,
you might as well have a nice day.
Why not keep on smiling while you
take the line of most resistance, even in LA?

A Note on Barber's *Adagio*

> . . . Back in Autumn 1963
Samuel Barber was alone and driving through
November rain in Iowa or Kansas.
When he turned on his radio he heard
them playing his *Adagio for Strings*.
Sick to death of his most famous composition,
he turned the dial through the static
until once again, and clearly—
The *Adagio for Strings*. When a third station, too,
and then a fourth, were playing it, he thought
he must be going mad. He turned off the radio
and stopped the car and got out by a fence
staring at the endless open space in front of him
where someone on a tractor plowed
on slowly in the rain. . .

The president had been assassinated
earlier that day, but Barber didn't know it yet.
He only knew that every station in America was playing
his *Adagio for Strings*.
He only knew he didn't know
why he should be responsible for such an ecstasy of grief.

For Dónal Gordon

Sadnesses: Black Seas

I

Tristia, tristia : Tomis or Constanța
Getae or Romanian might hear . . . might go and hide
heedless of a rhetoric resounding to its own

its onerous exemplum *adynata, adynata:* Naso
whose impossibilities would rage like Dido
hurling Latin in Aeneas' wake: O Divine Augustus

bitch of an apotheosis who recoiled, call, recall
those numbers moving with a grace that no one
south of Petersburg but Alexander Pushkin

could recite that song of bodies changing
into other bodies: Mandelstam prefiguring his own
departure into darkness gaudy indigence behind

beyond the poverty of happiness: eye of Eisenstein
plotting golden sections as caesurae thinking
two & three and two & three the empty baby carriage

bumping down Odessa steps the sly and hungry
host in naval whites at Yalta grinning at the crippled
president the portly flushed personified PM:

II

Tristia, tristia: adynata, adynata:
Scythians leap up from rocks look out from trees
as cameras grind in faithless documentary

and who can tell from just that word *departure*
how long spindles hum and shuttles flutter
back and forth to measure everything that's happened

happening again but this time without either
wax or bronze: *tristia, tristia:*
all the rivers flow back up to mountain streams

the horses of old Helios stumble in their course the sea's
aflame the plow of earth cleaves heaven:
General Insov was a loyal friend but what to do

with this new Governor Vorontsov good Ovidius
except go fuck his wife:
the field of honor is as boring as the gaming board:

adynata, adynata: Dr Smirnov will be shot close up
his pince-nez broken in his face if someone finds a man to play
the priest the sailors can be executed underneath a tarp

but what to do with all these little countries after such a scene
but swallow them: a ship might just as well
be named for Pushkin as Potemkin: Ovid has his statue now

and Stalin Churchill Roosevelt
it's true the birds are indiscriminate it's best no doubt
to be unknown a decent anonymity and

Mandelstam says women weave the men fall down in fields.

Tourists

My daughter writes to me from Athens:
Which wall was it you fell over here?
It wasn't Athens, it was Thessaloniki,
where I fell off the wall.

And into the sea, the wine-dark sea,
where she tells me on her card
she has been swimming. I had to dive
for my passport, wallet, glasses.

All the German and American and English
tourists laughed. I was a good sport
they said. I swam around the ferry pier
in coat and tie and shoes.

The wall in the postcard is the one
they stood the poet on to be shot.
There were no American or English tourists,
But all the Germans laughed.

He didn't swim around the ferry pier
in coat and tie and shoes.
He didn't dive for passport, wallet,
glasses. He just sank down to the bottom

And no one called him a good sport.

Photosonnets

On My Daughter's Orthodontic Self-Portrait, Age 12

Francis Bacon, I'd have said,
as if you'd ever seen a Francis Bacon!
And please, I thought, don't ever look
at anything by Diane Arbus. . . .

What you did was tell a friend to
point a Leica down your throat
as if it were a Luger . . . &
when you shouted *now,* to pull the trigger.

Then there is the other side of *scream*
you might call *smile,* the other
side of *walleyed* that you might call *focus.*

What you said ten years ago you'd call this thing
was *Stammer's Braces.*
On the back you wrote—*No, it's Cindy's Other Eye.*

On My Daughter's Portrait of Her Sister on a Bike, Age 13

The other side of bicycle is ghost, the other
side of ghost is maybe glasses.
Spectacles, one said. And when we lived in England
teachers would intone: *Now Cynouai,*

put your spectacles upon your nose!
The bicycle is negative and positive. Her sister, too.
One side black on white, the other white on black.
It's not ambivalence exactly; it isn't ambiguity;

it's double durability up in the attic in the trunk
and it's, I'd say, a speculative speech.
Can you catch a specter without spectrohelic specs?

1981: She's off to Church of England school
where they study species both Darwinian and Eucharistic.
She'll put her spectacles upon her nose.

A Civil Servant

Because the Muslims and the Hindus cannot
do this job, they turn to me—
a poor, impoverished Christian. They pay me
ten rupees each time, some fifty pence.

And look at this—one mud room, two beds,
a Pepsi calendar, a Coca-Cola
poster and the crucifix. My father, an
untouchable, cleaned the toilets in Lahore

and then converted. The British brought in
hanging with the cricket, but they
couldn't find a hangman. My father volunteered.
He'd rather hang a man than clean latrines.

They never tell me whom I'm going to hang.
They come and get me, or they send me
money for the bus or train. I'm the only
hangman in the country; I'm on call.

They got me up at 2 A.M. for Bhutto. It was
raining, and they brought him on a
stretcher. He wore the shalmar-kameez
and traditional long shirt. He was steady

as I fastened up the hood around his head
and then put round the noose. He didn't
say a word before I pulled the lever,
but somehow I was certain he was innocent.

I went home and drank all night and drank
so much I woke up in the wards with
alcoholic poisoning. They came to get me
there to hang the officers who gave

the evidence convicting Bhutto. They'd been
promised pardons but were being hanged

instead. They repudiated all their evidence
before I hanged them, one by one.

What kind of country is this anyway? I'm 65.
I've been the hangman here ever since my
father died. When they came to get me in the
wards, I told them I was far too sick to go.

But this is Pakistan. I'm Christian. So I went.

(Cutting. *Times* of London. Verbatim)

When Lilacs Last

Again I woke up frightened in the night
hearing shots from Leeper Park
where just a week ago the fourteen-year-old boy
shot the twelve-year-old.

And fifteen nervous senators won't support
an automatic weapons ban.
Streetsweepers. Parkblasters. Names
made up by someone with a job—

something no one sleeping down in Leeper Park has got.

The man who shielded his wife in San Francisco
by an elevator in a high rise office block
took a spray of bullets in his chest
from a former employee who'd got the sack.

I'm dying, he said. Kiss my son and daughter.

In the morning everything is quiet.
I walk outdoors and smell the lilac
billowing in waves over the rickety fence.

The men who sleep in Leeper Park
are waking up, and Lilac
is in bloom all over—even there.

Even in the front yard of the senator
who leans to the scent of it getting in his car
and sweetens for a moment
the sour business of his brokered vote.

Academic Poem

The headline says "A student
and his wife in double suicide . . ."
I read the article

hoping that it's not about someone I know.
It's not. It says that
Mr. A. S. Aptekar, an M.A. candidate

from India, "swallowed cyanide following
rejection Wednesday of his thesis."
So too his wife, and both of them left wills.

The paper says they also both left notes, that
both were "fully clothed
and on their bedroom floor" with Mr. Aptekar

"holding his wife in his arms."
And it's too late for me to do a thing.
It's too late to say, Please

Mr. Aptekar don't do it. Forget, Mr. Aptekar,
your silly thesis. Go back
to your village, let the sun shine on your face,

embrace your friends and kiss the earth
that bore you. Laugh aloud with
everyone about the habits of the comical Americans.

Walk beside the river flowing
to the Ganges and take off all your polyester clothes.
Lie down with your wife.

Hold her in your arms! but please don't
hold her like you're holding her right now because
of the rejection Wednesday of your thesis.

Get up off the floor, God damn it,
pack your bags, get out of here. We never want
to see your like again.

How obscene, how unspeakable and murderous
your kind of shame, how helpless
in our pity those of us who might have helped.

Persistent Elegy

(Shortly before the 1994 South African election my former
student, Clare Stewart, was murdered in KwaZulu,
probably by an Inkatha hit squad)

And now at last Nelson Mandela's elected.
But what of my student, Clare?
Would she have danced as she had expected?
They don't even number the dead in Rwanda.
She raises her hand in the air.
What did she do in KwaZulu to anger Inkatha?

She sits in my class long ago taking notes.
This is my student, Clare.
Volunteers have busily counted the votes.
She wakes to the voices of children.
Her daughter's among them there.
What did she do in KwaZulu to anger Inkatha?

No volunteers can describe what nobody sees.
She leaves a note in the mission.
She walks by the lake, the flowering trees.
Observers say the election is fair.
She gets in a pick-up, drives from the village.
She raises her hand in the air.

She tries to answer the question.
What did you do in KwaZulu to anger Inkatha?
What is the answer, Clare?
They don't even number the dead in Rwanda.
Nobody's counting there.
But what did she do in KwaZulu to anger Inkatha?

She raises her hand in the air.
And now at last Nelson Mandela's elected.
What of my student, Clare?
She never arrives where she is expected.
Everyone's weeping there.
What did she do in KwaZulu to anger Inkatha?

What of my student, what of my student, Clare?

My Mother's Webster

She'd never tell me how to spell a word;
Go look it up, she'd say. She'd say *It's there in Webster,*
pointing to the battered blue and dog-eared dictionary
that she'd lugged from Georgetown to Columbus long
before those Anglo-Saxon expletives she said offended her
entered the American Heritage. I find it at the bottom of a box
unpacking things I thought to save when she turned vague,

lost the words she'd loved, and started groping for a few
remembered monosyllables to get her through a day of
meals, treatments, therapies, and baths at Olentangy Home.
Her house is sold; she's 92; and I decide to look it up
when I'm unsure about how one spells *Houyhnhnm*
and want to write a footnote citing Swift in *Gulliver.*
The facing page is black with marginalia; it's in her hand.

What alchemy is this? *A curse on Sally Smothers*
she has written, circled, arrowed to *hostility*
in one direction, *hothead* in another. *Turn the page*
she writes, and there beside the underlined *horned toad*
and *hornet* she abbreviates, *S.S.*, with arrows to *horrendous.*
She writes: *My friends: Eleanor, Elizabeth, and Jean.*
She writes: *The boy I do not love: Jason Dean: ZZ.*

Some words are simply canceled: *housewife* with an X,
hooker with a line; the illustrations under *horseshoe*
toss her up to *horah*, ring her to *hosanna*; *horn of plenty* is
a *cornucopia*, and that is circled six or seven times.
Next to *horologe* she writes *ding-ding* and clearly likes
hornswoggle, prints in little caps: *They'll do it every time.*
She writes *I'll host a hostage in the hostel, my hors d'oeuvre!*

Who is this language sprite? It seems to be my mother
talking to herself in 1917. There's still heavy fighting on
the western front; her father has just died; she'll meet *my* father
in another seven years. There is no sulfa yet, no penicillin;
Eleanor and Jean will get the post-war flu and not survive.

I've never heard her mention Jason Dean. She will, in fact,
become a housewife and she'll outlive Sally Smothers

that old hothead she called *hornet* and *horned toad.*
The goddesses of seasons, Horae, might have taught her
in good time a ripe Horatian patience as she gazed
at *horoscope* and then *horizon*—looked up from the page
and out her bedroom window at the *horos,* boundary,
tangent plane across the surface of the globe defining
the conjunction of the earth and sky. She writes:

I guess that means about as far as I can see.
There's not a mark here or an indication that she saw her
future linked to *hospital* or *hospice*—
nor to *Houyhnhnms,* rational and gentle creatures
one might like for neighbors even at the Olentangy Home
and whose name I cannot spell. I can hear her say again
Well go and look it up, It's there in Webster,

meaning this particular blue book, and not some other.
I'd look her up herself if I could find her. She's always in,
but she is never there. She's here in 1917 and not hornswoggled
or intimidated or a hostage in some hostel where they
do it every time. There's a horseshoe on her door.
There's not a single cloud on the horizon and it's June.
She'll be her own hors d'oeuvre and dance the horah round

a horn of plenty. She writes: *I'm Thirteen in Three Days.*

The Singing

Now we could talk. Too late,
too long ago I see you
in that chair and see
myself unwilling and impatient

and so full of hurry that I
hurt to get away and say
some quick and careless thing
which turns out to be all

I managed as the final words
I spoke to you. But now,
now we could talk. I have grown
patient. I sit as you once sat

alone most days and stare at nothing.
I know—too late, too well—what
you might say, or rather might have said,
what I will never now respond to you

but only mutter to myself or into darkness.
It sounds like sorrow. I mean the sound
of it is sorrow as some kind of song.
It's not so much a saying, then, as singing?

Did you want to sing to me that day
some twenty years ago, for me to sing to you?
Dear God what kind of song? What sorrow
sings what wretchedness to bed?

You did not go to bed. You sat. Your heart.
More rest from sitting up all night
than lying down. And all night long you sang.
Sang only to yourself because

there's no one ever who will listen
to such song. I know. I sing.

We'd sing that song together if you
were alive—the only one you sang,

the only one I sing beneath what talk
I can what tense I cannot manage
knowing far too late too well how long
you sat in what was never silence

what was never anything but song.
Now we could talk. Now we'd keep our silence
perfectly and hear each other sing.
Your past my future in that present when

impatient I heard nothing and went out.

Left Hands and Wittgensteins
for Roy Fisher at Seventy and, inter alios, Leon Fleisher, Blaise Cendrars

Paul's brother Ludwig the philosopher had said
the world is everything that is the case
in case you lost your arm. In case you could not play
for all the world. *No left hand*
we used to say as glib precocious critics of the young
Ahmad Jamal, one of us the southpaw pitcher
on the high school baseball team who struck out every
righthand batter in the junior league.
But Paul was *all* left hand who bitched at both Ravel
and Sergei Prokofiev but nonetheless
performed their music no right hand would ever play.
The world was everything that was the case
when Blaise Cendrars also lost his arm. In that same war.
In that same war where everything that was the case
exploded in the world. My friend the southpaw pitcher studied
in the end with Leon Fleisher who awoke one day
with no right hand as a result of carpal-tunnel stress. A syn-
drome: drone, his repertory was diminished but he played
Prokofiev he played Ravel, and all thanks due to Wittgenstein
whose world was everything that was the case.

Left hand, left wing? Roy, are all right-handers Tories
in their bones? They'd case your joint as if
they'd lost most everything left in the world.
(Or would you pack them in your case with all the world
except for B and exit in that key?) I weep
for your right arm, your stroked-out days of therapy,
your egging on your brain to find a few more millimeters
of its limb. But what's permission but commission
to a left-hand poet, left-hand pianist at seventy?
You might well go ask Wittgenstein, might well ask Cendrars.
Then go ahead—put the piano at risk, put the poem
in jeopardy: Millennium's a comin' after, Roy:
If anything could be the case
the world is everything that is the case.
Are those iambs, da-dah da-dah? Is that in 4/4 time?

C.P.R.

Poem after poem I've written to you, love,
songs and foolish valentines,
curt demanding notes, confused apologies and

poems in the mind I dare not show you
or write down, their praise
of you so pornographic that they'd

set the eye aflame or burn the hand
that touched them. Wife,
mistress, sister, mother of my lives and lines,

one after the other for these thirty years,
now three days a week you visit
the Red Cross on Jefferson and learn

techniques no prosodist dare dream of
or any *Kama Sutra* recommend. Oh, I know—
you've saved my life before, time

after time, life after life, each time
more difficult the life that's saved, more
difficult the act of saving it. This

cold heart of mind—now you'd pound it back
to beating for you if you had to.
And how unkind if I could not respond!

A letter from my cousin says her husband
"died peacefully in his sleep." He wasn't even sick!
If I must die, I'd rather die awake

and staring in amazement while you filled my lungs
with all the air your lungs could gasp
and pounded on my chest

in just and utter outrage over what I'd done.

The Lyric Suite: Aldeburgh Festival, Snape

Consummate in sound, *appassionato,*
Alban Berg's unconsummated love for Werfel's sister!
Her initials, H and F, conjoined with his own
as in a page illuminated in the mind
from *Kells* or Lindisfarne, locked to Schoenberg's mathematics.
Hanna's copy of the score alone
sang the unsung text, penciled in and set
but then erased. The quote from *Tristan.*
Then the *De Profundis Clamavi* of Baudelaire.

How alien this passion sounds arching out of Hanna's Prague
of 1925 and into evening mists of a tranquil Suffolk summer,
weaving through the reeds around the Alde
and reaching on towards Orford church to dissipate
like unfulfilled desire.
And yet how I desire you, listening and failing
to listen to this sound, drifting
on a music of my own, then returned abruptly to this hall
by stricture and precision.

Allegretto gioviale . . . and the theme,
the twelve-tone row, enclosed by her initials.
"No hint," he wrote, "of tragedy to come."
Near us here, the old mill at Letheringham
is still. The wheel turned the year they wrote
the Doomsday Book. I've known this landscape
now for twenty years, felt it utterly
suffused with the presence of the woman here
beside me. Heavy rain this morning
sent the peahens scurrying, a huddle of ducks
and guinea fowl disappearing among reeds.
Daffodils were thick along the stream.
A tree trunk full of moss. Small brick cottage,
dull red tiles on its roof. . . . I sit
beside the woman I have loved for twenty years.
I think of someone else.

I think of you, and I desire you, listening
and failing to listen to this sound,
as he desired you himself, straining for the boundary
of expression as the spindle of his time unwound,
listening and failing to listen
to the voices of Vienna, generations of them
singing in a thousand violins, all those
strings attached to every note he wrote, every string
played pizzicato saying *du du du*
and meaning *her,* and yet he too desired you,
wrote his program into what I hear
and do not hear, writing letters with his other hand
to say *I was unfaithful to you only during*
a performance of the Mahler, only
because Mahler took my mind from you, my love,
but only for an hour, thinking really *Hanna, Hanna,*
whom he called Mopinka, and his program,
amoroso, then *misterioso* and *ecstatico....*

And why should not your name be Hanna? since
I cannot name you? since you have today no other name?
since I think of you as *thou* but need to call
out now, to call out and to whisper both, to call
you by some name, to whisper in the silence between
movements *Do you hear the singing now?* to be assured
that no one does, and not to mean do you,
do *you* hear it who are part of it as word and sound,
nor in any way confuse you with my love,
my love, linking your initials in some page
illuminated in the mind from *Kells* or Lindisfarne—
Hanna, then, Mopinka.

Do you hear the singing now? But now there is no singing,
was no singing but for those who heard it
in imagination, two of them and two of us....
She shakes her head, and in the space between
the *presto delirando* and the *largo*
landscape opens from the hall beside the Alde
and into time. A secret name, and an acknowledged name,
inhabit it. And are there always two?

The mill stream at Letheringham flows beneath
the wheel, the Alde by Snape and Iken,
then below the Orford castle keep and to the sea.
Water fowl leave their hieroglyphic prints
on mud as slick as oil while the tidal river shrinks
into a ribbon and the boats lie crazily
at angles in the ooze and weeds. Darkness comes
to Tunstall Forest, Campsea Ash and Woodbridge.
Again the quartet plays, *desolato* now.

My cry arises from a landscape with no brook
or tree, no field or flock, where air is lead and where
in shadows terror looms. . . . As if some tenor
might emerge from such a place and stretch his voice
four octaves on the rack of *Fleurs du Mal . . .*
The cold terror of this icy star . . . and of this
night . . . So slowly does
the spindle of our time unwind . . . When all is done
we do what is expected, clap our hands
and shuffle up the aisle while four musicians,
after bows, pack up instruments and leave the quiet hall.
Berg's Helene listened to this suite one summer night
some sixty years ago. Who knows what she heard?
She spoke of neither fear nor of desire.
When all was done, she did what was expected,
clapped her hands and shuffled
up the aisle while the four musicians,
after bows, packed up instruments and left the quiet hall,
so slowly did the spindle of their time unwind.

And now the landscapes cease
to alternate, to overlap: Prague returns to Prague,
Vienna to Vienna, and I am here in Suffolk by the Alde.
I walk away in moonlight like some dizzy Pierrot,
some Pierrot Lunaire. . . .
Beside me there is just one woman,
steady and serene—
and silent as the silent endless last indifferent sky.

Pages

from a book of years

Pages from a Book of Years
Part One
· · ·
I

1959. And underneath the photographs
names of people you can count

as if they numbered works and days
and years: one and one by one

become again these Davids, Joels & Fayes
and 1959's about to flower

flame again to 1960, 1961

The flower in the flame. The fame of that. Those days. People you could count who
counted then. David, Joel and Faye; Margaret, Ann, and Margaret-Ann; Sondra,
Bonnie, Lisa, Lennie, Kaye. Luck (o sister life) you'd think was little more than win-
ning dashes, listening to the jazz at Marty's 502, kissing Cora with your left hand up
her skirt in that black and battered Studebaker Lark. Boris Pasternak, I'd say. I'll bet
not one of you has read a word by Boris Pasternak. I didn't mean his novel. Sister
Life, I'd say. I loved the title, hadn't read the poems. My Sister Life. I'd run until I felt
like I could fly, then stand under ice-cold showers for an hour. The tingle of well-
being being well inside the brackets of a decade for another several months

whose year whose yearbook opens really. On your lap.

Who'd say Nadir How Now Restless Wind or Endine Tim Tam Quil and Gallant
Man what's Bold Ruler Oligarchy Jewel's Reward? If horses were wishes, what's your
wish: To winter in Kentucky, summer in Saratoga.

Rook-and-queen your combination in a close, coming back against the dragon varia-
tion of a Russian's elegant Sicilian.

Khrushchev in New York. His phrase for the occasion not a quote you'd look up in a
book by Boris P. His rook not named for Tim Tam, nor his queen for Nadir. In the
rulers' table names decline like sentences beneath the photographs that you could
count as Dave and Joel and Faye: King Saud is sand and Faisal backs to Franco
Gamal Abdel Nasser turns to Eisenhower Pope John Ho Chi-minh

David Goss and Pham Van-dong
Joel & Bonnie

Margaret, Ann, and Margaret-Ann
One & one by one

in time you do forget well almost all of it the whole damn thing goes almost blank

goes wholly blank in time

for Governor-General Viscount Charles John Lyttelton Cobham, say.

II

Disasters 1959: Rio de Janeiro plane crash
Guadalajara bus and train Formosa

earthquake Istanbul a fire Western
Pakistan a flood & in the Persian Gulf typhoons

a caved-in mine in Merlebach and just
northeast of Newfoundland a sunken ship,

Blue Wave

I put my hand directly up her skirt and she did not say no don't do it didn't say a thing
and so I kept it there a moment just above the knee and then began advancing slowly
with my finger tips in little steps

blue wave, blue wave

And out there somewhere Viscount Charles John Lyttelton Cobham.

This year Raymond Chandler died and so did Abbott's friend Costello. It's hard to
think of Abbott all alone his eyes upon Costello's derby hanging on the hatrack in the
hall. For days you keened in grief for Errol Flynn your only child's Robin. General
Marshall, Admiral William Halsey also on the list. And Ike in tears. Who'd say weep
my love for

John Foster Dulles

Amy's mother Florence Smith

                     For every day there's death you've got to chronicle
and someone writes the years in yearbooks puts eventually the volumes in a right and
goodly order on the shelf

who loved her best friend Amy's mother Florence Smith.

Joel and I would play this game called Scrounge. Others I've discovered called it
Bernie-Bernie. You could lose a lot of money and a number of our friends and victims
did. After dropping all his cash one night Carl Butler put his watch into the pot and
then his shoes. Who the hell would want your shoes said Joel. They're first-rate shoes
said Carl. They're ordinary Keds said Joel so what's about them so first-rate. Anyway
he lost these too and then he went home barefoot. The music that we listened to was
jazz: Monk and Miles, the MJQ, Dave Brubeck. It all seemed so subversive. We'd
smoke, play cards, listen to the jazz, take the watches and the shoes of our acquain-
tances, engage in repartee appropriating everything we could from what we dimly
understood to be a demi-monde of jazzmen and hipsters.

Actapublicorist entered dictionaries. Tokodynamometer and Turbofan.

When I got my hand inside her pants she said You know I never did let anybody do
that and I'm pretty sure you shouldn't be the first. She stares out of her photograph.
Going on eighteen and still a virgin just like all the rest of us and everyone we knew.

III

In four hours three minutes fifty-two point two seconds Anatoly Vedykov walked for
50,000 meters. As for ourselves, we set no records. Neither at the gallop or the trot or
the canter. Times got worse, we stayed out longer in the nights playing Scrounge or
waiting for the final set at Marty's 502. I started calling 502 my distance. What's your
distance? 440, right? In fact I've taken up the 502. After one jaunt around the oval
feeling pretty good about my winnings on the night before I ran directly into Larson
who had evidently clocked me. Christ, he said, you might as well have walked

the last four hundred yards with Anatoly Vedykov.

By 1960 you'd have heard
them all at Marty's: Monk and Miles, Coltrane,

Horace Silver, Sonny Rollins, even now and then
a white man like Giuffre.

I liked Giuffre, the strange sound of his trio. I
thought of it as 50,000 meters worth of walking music for the likes of Anatoly
Vedykov. Larson used to play the records in the locker room incanting 440 502, 440
502. It must have seemed occult to anyone but us.

Trav'lin Light: studies in the application of La Violette's idea of slow-motion counter-
point. And then as JG said: because we're trav'lin round the country in a light Volk-
swagen bus and very light ourselves (minus bass and drums, & minus keyboard).

Giuffre alternating clarinet & tenor sax
Brookmeyer's valve trombone
Jim Hall: guitar

Pickin' 'em up and layin' 'em down.

In slow-motion counterpoint: Charles Van Doren
answers questions on TV inside a concentration booth:

Khrushchev bangs his shoe in the UN: Five to four
the Court upholds the power of Congress

to investigate subversives: Ingemar Johansson
knocks out Floyd Patterson: Joel Montgomery

spells correctly *fanfaronade*: Vanguard II is launched
to orbit for 100 years: Bobby Fisher turns 16.

The quiz show scandal was a revelation to the gullible: Van
Doren, like the others, given answers in advance. Who'd fight the Swede? who'd take
off a shoe with old Nikita? Bobby Fisher's rook-and-queen against a dragon variation
of Sicilian would spell fanfaronade in any bee. Or Fanfandango. Farondole.

Had we not discovered Scrounge we might have found a game of fan-tan at the Olen-
tangy Village Chinese restaurant: beans, coins, & counters in some hidden place. By
1961 Anatoly Vedykov would still be walking. Explorer VI: fallen from the sky.

IV

Between your visits to the nursing home you burrow into all the secret delves of what was once your house, turning up most anything: decomposing diaries; a list of cities where you thought you'd like to live; names for the year that has locked you in its book

on the Serengeti plain of Tanganyika or the streets of new Havana or the Himalayas in Nepal. Year of the Missing Link year

of Fidel & Che year
of Edmund Hillary, of Anatoly Vedykov.

San Francisco Paris Rome or Venice Leningrad Palermo in Granada Prague Vienna Perpignan Southend-on-Sea Tangier

        or anywhere but here.

All your letters from the time you first left home and went to summer camp.
A thousand cancelled checks.
Poor Aunt Peggy's glasses labelled with a tie-on tag.

When Leakey found his skull our anthropology consisted of examining the heads we knew already frozen in the permafrost of photographs and checking the cephalic index: broad or long, no one looked entirely human. Had the photographer asked everyone to smile and say *Zinjanthropus* he couldn't have done better: a class of 1959 emerging one by one from some preconscious primate's shadow just in time for a production of *The King and I* whose star Yul Brynner clone would take up mortuary science.

Smile and say Zinjanthropus.
See you in Tangier.

        Or in Santiago in the eastern Oriente provence or in Santa Clara in Las Vilas. First the local victories. Then an armored column moving on Havana. In the thinnest air, Edmund Hillary's on Mt. Makulu in Nepal. At 20,000 feet there's no sign of Yeti. You sign your name and sign your name again. The checks, the powers of attorney, living wills. You find the bottom lines and cross your t's.

Take me home she said don't sell the house I can't remember quite which one you are you know I really don't live here I'm only visiting.

Batista's visiting Dominican Republic. The Dalai Lama's visiting Bombay.

At 20,000 feet you can scarcely breathe at all.

We shaved his head in turns and eventually he was completely bald. He'd sing and dance. He'd wear the costume Mrs. Orr designed herself to much applause. In twenty years he'd get his thin embalmer's hands on Mrs. Orr and Miss Kirkpatrick, on Mrs. Jones and Mr. Michelson and Mr. Todd. He'd stand discretely at the edge of things while those of us who still were left in town would pay our last respects. He'd give your mother your Aunt Peggy's glasses labelled with a tie-on tag.

He'd hang Costello's derby on the hatrack in the hall.

V

Old hat millineries made their mark:
the derby was a hit. Also slouch, fedora, swagger,

even Cossack. Down at the heel you'd find a dangerous spike,
you'd see a leopard stole, then an otter trench,

maybe even Jules François Crahay the man himself.
Hobble skirt. And after Fashion, Finland.

K.A Fagersholm had fallen. R. Buckminster Fuller next.
Geodesic domes for radar on the DEW Line.

Distant Early Warning scanned the millenary sky.

When teleologists took Alpha from our almanac, Omega wept. Rebel hit-men on the margin became hatters. Barkan, Binkley, Bowen, Cash; Giles, Goss and Griffin. What were they to Advertising, Aeronautics? Taken from aback, Zoetrope and Zero; but underneath the photographs such confidence: Not a single future written off as bankrupt. Nor as death from aneurysm. Not a battered bride. These who'd be the doctor lawyer businessmen and engineers demand a potency beyond their prime and potentate. Look at Shah Mohammed smiling warmly from his page. Why ever should he not? He married young Queen Farah in December and is hoping for a male heir

as Lunik III observes the far side of the moon and Don Fidel the progress of a hundred executions in a single hot and humid afternoon.

Throw, the saying goes, your hat into the ring

                                    but first you put your tennis shoes
into the pot. Only then to leave, broke and barefoot, your corner table at the 502 for
Cora's house at twelve, head all full of Bird and Monk and Miles. She'd be waiting
there all right, standing at the doorway in her shorts and bathed entirely in yellow
light. You felt like Edmund Hillary at 20,000 feet.

Or like Costello's derby hanging in the hall.

A darker horse than Sister Life had never won a race. If David Lean could feast a few
years later on Zhivago and convince Omar Sharif he was a poet, I could dance my Sis-
ter to the Millenary Ball and call her Cor (a.k.a. Omega Alpha). There we'd make the
milliners all eat their hats. Dave Goss ate his hat. And Stephen Husted ate one. Harry
Cash consumed a blue beret. Ruth McCallister nibbled at a pill box daintily. Randy
Miller and his friend Sam Woodruff both ate busbies while our future General Pat-
ton, off to West Point in the fall, broke a tooth off on his helmet.

You thought, of course, the future would be yours—as did Che and JFK. Instead
you'd be the future's, which would make a meal of you. One and one by one to cower
in its flame as works and days unnumber and you do forget well almost all of it the
whole damn thing gone blank in time and you too on the list with Raymond Chan-
dler Errol Flynn and Amy's mother Florence Smith. Blue wave.

Tokodynamometer, my love, and Turbofan. Amen. Far out on the plain of Tan-
ganyika. A pair of glasses labelled with a tie-on tag. A scattering of Pesos, Drachmas,
Yen.

Part Two

. . .

I

America First or Lend-Lease. 1941.
The Christmas holidays at last and New Year's Eve.

How to measure now and
then and now again and in the mind

or then as now for all of them in kin & kind.
And how conceive.

How to parse out features in a body of the past
that took its measures . . .

Among the old prescriptions, bottles, and bandaids, *Married Love* (of 1936) moulders in
a cabinet. Illustrated in a modest way for the fastidious, it's clear enough: and you your-
self the end of all instruction and a digit added to the census come September. They'd
listen to a fireside chat like everybody else. They'd sit beside their radio and smoke their
Lucky Strikes. No Third Term they'd chanted with their friends. They're quiet now

listening to a man before the network microphones adjusting his pince-nez. He
speaks the words Great Arsenal. He tries out fear: Spies already walk the streets of
Washington. He says you cannot reason with incendiary bombs, and looks into the
eyes of Carole Lombard sitting there with twenty others who have jammed into the
little room to hear this live. Your father stands, walks out to the kitchen porch and
looks up at the sky trying to imagine what it's like in London. Your mother's think-
ing of that night they danced to Jimmy Dorsey's band.

Or Paul Whiteman. Maybe Guy Lombardo, called by *Down Beat* magazine the King
of Corn. In the photograph you turn up in the desk, they stand beside their old De
Soto parked beside the north-east corner of the house. First car. First house.

First war to be entirely theirs. The last was for the eldest
not the younger sons. For Edward, say, who sits alone in darkness

in a corner of the old Glen Echo house unvisited.
Doughboy with the Spanish flu, then encephalitis, he'd dance

to Guy Lombardo if he could but he can barely stand;
his walk's a kind of shuffle when he walks.

Named for his father who had ridden San Juan Hill
with Teddy R, the name came down on you

like some genetic ton of bricks: johnEdward. Edward.
Edward Edward Edward . . .

But then you're not a part of all this yet. It's only New Year's Eve. Great Arsenal is still
a phrase and not a thousand tanks, not a bill before the house, not a wound to Charles
Lindbergh, hero isolationist, who'd flown so far it seemed so long ago.

II

They'd listen to Jack Benny once a week. Brought to you by Jell-O. They'd go out to the
films: Errol Flynn and Ronald Reagan chased John Brown to Harpers Ferry; Abbott
got so angry that he made Costello cry. Rosebud someone told them was the codename
for a German agent, not what William Randolph Hearst had called his mistress's

obscene that word if you can think of it Louella Parsons
Hedda Hopper said and recommended censorship

in time of war
a cenogenesis for every member cenobitical

eventually a cenotaph erected
in your own back yard with every name

you'd carve on every tall Glen Echo oak
in stone

Rosebud? Tricycle in fact.
Turned by MI5 to double on the Lisbon Abwehr, Dusko Popov brought his microdot
to Hoover at the FBI who didn't get the import of the drawings questions diagrams
regarding ammunition dumps the hangars installations on the wharf the workshops
dry docks airfields naval operations in Hawaii. After Benny, newsman Walter
Winchell trashed the *glowering boy the sullen tot of history the corn-fed Spengler stalking
through the family dining room with clouded brow a darkling child at our feast.* Your
mother thought he should be president; your father thought he should be shot. He
flew so far it seemed so long ago.

59

This year Scott Fitzgerald died and Henri Bergson Kaiser Wilhelm Joyce Virginia
Woolf and Robert Baden-Powell the founder of the Boy Scouts. Sherwood Anderson
Tagore and Robert Bridges also on the list with Lou Gehrig and the voice of Earle
Graser known to every child as The Lone Ranger. It's hard to think of Graser's horse
without a rider someone on a soundstage horseshoes in his hands who'd gallop them
beneath the microphone on sand and sawdust spread out in a box. Who'd say weep
my love for

Nazi aces Mölders and Udet
the Prussian officer the SS Einsatzgruppen shot outside of Leningrad. Tsvetayeva got
through to Moscow then to Pasternak at Peredelkino to Pasternak who didn't say you
will be safe right here my poet stay with me my love I'll call you Sister Life. She
hanged herself and three days later I was born.

That would be September. Now they measure bauxite for incendiaries chromium for
armor plate copper for de-gaussing apparatuses to use against magnetic mines mag-
nesium and manganese for alloys

lead tin nickel zinc and tungsten.

They went out to the corner deli for dessert walking back along the old Glen Echo
drive where icy branches of the winter trees clicked against each other silvering in
moonlight. That night Edward died. And RKO let Kane sit on the shelf three
months even though the word was out on Rosebud. Densko Popov said my name is
Densko Popov and I've come from Lisbon on my tricycle to help you break their codes.

III

97-shiki O-bun In-ji-ki J-machine
a rat's baffle cry for cryptanalysis

a rising son whose father came from Kishinev
to sell them on how well the Singer sewed

sold them measurements of matrices
enciphering a system of successive

polyalphabetic substitutions and the wonder was
DiMaggio had fifty hits

in fifty games with everybody in the country counting and the wonder was the Brits had cracked Enigma too at Bletchley Park as Bertolt Brecht settled into Hollywood. Three years later I would ride my yellow tricycle round and round the dining table while the old Victrola played out *McNamara's Band*. When the music went all sour I'd dismount and turn the crank until I couldn't turn it any more. McNamara gave them twenty records when he learned about the pregnancy and one of them was *McNamara's Band*.

Meet Marlene Dietrich, Peter Lorre, Thomas Mann, Stravinsky: Yamamoto wearing his enciphered purple robes. Codename Fixer. Codename Trickster. Fliegerhauptmann Lindbergh. Fliegerhauptmann Hess.

That year measured distance by unusual means. Home plate to left field wall, degree of arc required to hook a fist in Billy Conn's protesting open mouth, miles south from Flynn's estate to child prostitute and Nazi agent in a single room, leagues required to get your sea legs on the exile ship as sonar signals rippled out in waves. Fliegerhauptmann thought he saw the coast of Scotland, looped his Messerschmitt, and parachuted down before the unbelieving eyes of Piers the plowman standing there at dusk near Eaglesham who'd take a measure more than Lindbergh's take a measure rather less than Hess.

He caught the outside curve and drove it to the wall He bloodied him at last and down he went like Schmeling smartass whiteboys come on quiet nights to lose their innocence He put his hand directly up her skirt and she did not say no don't do it didn't say a thing and so He turned the crank until he couldn't turn it any more and put on *McNamara's Band*.

He touched her rosebud it was manganese in alloy
it was allies it was axis
when she hanged herself and three days later you were born

like all these other codes and secret agents—
works of days apocalyptical foreseen by even Catalan Ramon
who spun configured mysteries on interlocking disks

to make an *ars inventiva veritatis* of the nine attributes of God.

Rat's baffle cry who'd haiku now DiMaggio my hero Errol Flynn my Messerschmitt my Spirit of St. Louis and by Louis's right cross and uppercut *Yo no naka wa jigoku no ue no hanami kana* : world's middle
                        walking on the roof of hell
                                  and flower gazing!

IV

Kata kana over purple and in open code the short-wave-east-wind-rain. Yamamoto: Does it seem as if the birth is immanent? *Higashi No Kaze Ame*. It had been a healthy boy brought to term in all good time who'd twist the dials of his interlocking disks or ride a yellow tricycle around his room to wind up magic blow the east wind back uncloud the dark horizon that a hard rain down could never rain. He'd made an *ars inventiva veritatis* of the nine attributes of God

he'd walk the dog. Dog days. Dogtooth violets fringing sidewalks in his neighborhood. Long ago his Mendelian studies of the polypeptide chains. Who'd gazed on flowers walked the roof of hell and at his back heard echoes from Atlantic wolf packs answering their kin in kind: No kata kana haiku now or Yamamoto open code but lost sailors whispering *Jeder Engel ist schrecklich*.

Angels danced on conning towers, flight decks, the tips of wings. Fast tödliche Vögel.

McNamara had this problem with his inner ear. He said I think we'll just use Navahos or Cherokees the way the Brits have used Maltese. No one understands a wretched word of it. I'm so unsteady I can barely walk but still the beauty of it is I won't be draftable and neither I should think will you with that rheumatic heart. They slept through Bach at Disney's new *Fantasia*. They even slept through Rimsky-Korsakov and Chernobog Triumphant who would terrify you in due time and make you cry. Fast tödliche Engel. You'd hold your mother's hand.

These two buddies never went to war. They didn't have the heart for it, they didn't have the ear. They dug up McNamara's yard to plant tomatoes and zucchini where I'd help them pull up weeds in '45. They planted cantaloupe and carrots and potatoes. Their blushing melons and their apprehensive wives grew big all summer long decoding Mendel's laws. Mandrake Europe shrieked in Chernobog's right hand and Disney loosed the FBI on Hollywood. *The place was full of lousy Communists and they were worse than Nazis and the Japs. Even my friend Eisenstein who'd shaken hands with Mickey went back home to Moscow fawning over Stalin like a daffy duck.*

Early August and die Vögel gazing down at Leningrad:
Walpurgis Nacht conducted by the Wehrmacht.

Sedarim read out Haggadah the 14th of Nisan
but every path of exodus was cut.

Every angel terrified. Every angle squared.

Every square enciphered as a circle.

You could sing like Chaliapin you could fight like Alexander Nevsky but you might as well lie doggo and just pray for snow like Sergei Mikhailovich in Alma Alta. Tapping on his telegraph in Kinderspiele calling USA he'd whisper
Uncle Walt!
I look around me now and somehow think I see you in this fire
all your totems and your metamorphoses. Animism here's our way of life.

Every loaf of bread we bake can creep away.
Every stone along the narrow streets can mock us.

Every mouse that's left alive can weep.

V

One and one by one. The flower in the flame.
The manganese and armor plate and tungsten.

They went out to the corner deli walking back along the old Glen Echo Drive and then she thought she felt the first contractions. Someone on a soundstage with horseshoes in his hands would gallop there beneath a microphone on sand and sawdust spread out in a box. Horse without a rider. He'd said to her one day you will be safe right here my poet stay with me my love I'll call you Sister Life.

Hiding in the vast Pacific swells were *Zuikaku* and *Akagi* while the old fusilier who would speak to you one day, shell shocked from the other war and neurasthenic, stood not far from Dover among failing numina of kin and kind looking for an efficacious sign.

Higashi No Kaze Ame. Jeder Engel ist schrecklich.

When teleologists put Alpha in their almanac, Omega danced. Rebel hit-men on the margin got their hammers. Disney, Lindbergh, Louis, Flynn; Benny, Abbott, Hopper. What were they to Aachen, Aaron's rod? Taken from aback, Zipangu and Zion; and underneath the photographs such confidence: Not a single future written off to buzzbombs. Nor as death from Zyklon. Not a battered bride. Those who'd be the doctor lawyer businessmen and unacknowledged legislators all demand a potency beyond their prime. Look at young Johannes smiling from his page. Why ever should he not? He married Miss Kirkpatrick last December and is hoping for a male heir.

Take me home she said don't sell the house I can't remember quite which one you are you know I really don't live here I'm only visiting. God is subtle He is not malicious Einstein said and Eisenstein of Chernobog He is a code. They show them movies in the nursing home. I know when I was born but can't remember how it felt.

When they bought their blackout curtains down at Woolworth's McNamara took his box of wooden nickels from a shelf and buried it among the blackened frosted melons in his garden. You could also blast your lithium with deutrons and irradiate your mercury for gold. You could sign up with Enrico Fermi and get rich on U-235.

You could dance with her to Guy Lombardo
look at all the photographs drive the old De Soto down the streets of 1941
and knock out Billy Conn.
You could sell the yellow tricycle to Densko Popov sew a shroud on Singer push the Lend-Lease bill in Congress measure bauxite for incendiaries split the atom drop the bomb dismantle DNA and find a proper setting for the cenotaph.
But that won't bring Lou Gehrig up to bat or put a Ranger in the empty silver saddle.

Zeros were reported flying in the skies above L.A. Alphas and Omegas over San Francisco. Take me home she said don't sell the house I can't remember quite which one you are you know I really don't live here I'm only visiting.

One and one by one remembers quite and who you were
Rerhüf, Retarf, Retam, Otomamay . . .
                              Visiting.
Alphas and Omegas on their way to Aachen.
Zipangu and Zion.
                  Noiz Noiz.   U   gnp   z.

Part Three

. . .

I

Russian MIGs & Mau Maus. Dead Sea scrolls & Piltdown men.
You heard they'd executed Beria.
They'd execute the Rosenbergs, but not the ones you knew.

That girl in World History came down with Polio.
Or was it Civics? Or did she get TB?
In 1953 we got TV. Nearly everyone we knew already had it.

His joke the year before when we were still the last among our friends to get it was to point me down the basement stairs and say I got us one go have a look—at the Bendix, it turned out, spinning water down its drain to end the cycle and my mother smiling there about to hang my shirts and sheets and underclothes up on the line. But politics had forced his hand eventually: he'd wanted Joe McCarthy in his living room and so I got Lucille Ball and he got Roy Cohn and all of us got *Dragnet* and the Coronation. I also got a camera with a flash attachment that would make me popular with Ned's precocious sister Nell.

You wanta kiss my sister?

_____?

I'd take her picture though. Let's do fashion shots, she'd often say. She must have been fifteen. She must have shown you Ralph Marino silhouettes, Mollie Parnis satin collars, Skinner crepes, Dior's Maxime with folded cummerbund and cinching narrow waist with deep and strapless décolletage. This, she'd say, is my bodice. And this is my breast. You'd flash your bulb.

More fraudulent than your pornography the Piltdown find as printed once again in glossy mags—that skull, that jaw. *Eoanthropus dawsoni* took no oath with Adam Mumbi and Gikuyu but his spectographic studies conjured Mau Mau out of Aramaic for the deuterocanonical echt deutsch.

Who'd cast Doris Day as Ethel Rosenberg? Who'd present
to Eisenhower Beria's pince-nez?
Stern declension down this year as Jim Thorpe died

and Dylan Thomas Robert Taft Prokofiev Picabia
and Uncle Max of natural causes
more or less and only Julius & Ethel on the list electrocuted Beria just shot.

That year all nephology seemed neomorphic all neology unneighborly: Communists might also be good citizens said Mrs. Lynch who lost her job for telling us just that when she had finished reading us aloud that Mayakovsky play *A Cloud in Pants*.

And on the new TV such news: his list of enemies identified in government his hand upraised his posse a Poseidon of a force his posture so remote from hers who came to us from London on that tiny screen and was anointed with the oils from a gold ampulla with a tiny spoon. *Te Deum Laudamus* they sang. Regalia were passed around and they arrayed her with Colobium Sidonis and then handed her the spurs the orb the ring the sceptre with the cross the rod and dove. Her photograph sped round the world
but Nell's I hid away. Sherpa Tensing near the top of Everest, I took the south col dreaming of Nepal.

II

You'd play at mountaineering down in what the others called *the glen* but you called *the ravine* because your parents did. You'd also do the Bedouins exploring Dead Sea caves. You'd do Korean War and Mau Mau massacres. Along the Khumbu Glacier up the icefall hacking steps and fixing ropes, you'd pull up Ned who'd fall exhausted in your arms at over 20,000 feet. You'd make your camp and wait until the lovers came in cars.

It may be the Essenes invented Satan
but my father thought it was Supreme Court Liberals

like Douglas who'd reverse him and his colleagues on appeal.
He too was Supreme, but only in Ohio,

"sitting on the bench" like some poor third string guard.
He'd sup on his suppositories. Our cave had

turned up parchments wrapped like mummies in old earthen jars
& we found psalms, beatitudes, sundry sapiential works

and Messianic rules. Also a Masonic ring we traded to the Brits
for their binoculars.
.... *ytlh 'nšym hyym, wtlytmh 'wtw 'l h's wymt*—
He hangs the men alive! You shall hang him on the tree and he shall die. For passing information to an enemy, e.g. For delivering one's people up: *Epikataratos pas ho kre-*

mamenos epi xylou. And then we found the spoons and buttons, needles, nails, & coins. We found a dildoe and a dilly bag. Between your visits to the nursing home the CIA declassifies Venona: now you know Antenna Calibre and Goose were agents back in Babylon and Tyre.

                      & in the drawers & closets of your mother's house those spoons and buttons from the cave. Also baseball cards and Marvel comic books, Qumran's pesharim, letters from Antenna, photographs of Nellie as Maxime.

Among the word lists for a new vocabulary circa new half-century you'd chainjack way downrange a firestorm's megadeath.
You'd back-breed in 3-D at burnout speed.

Ethel ran the deli down on Hudson Street beside the movie house my mother called "the picture show." That's Ethel *Rosenberg*. Neighbors asked her if she knew the other one the atom spy or if she'd change her name or did she know Klaus Fuchs and all those others in the news. She'd drop a bagel in your dilly bag without so much as saying Old Los Alamos although she'd whisper in your ear non sequitur's tautologies. Sunset over the ravine as Red Chinese and North Koreans climbed up Pork Chop Hill.

We'd dug in deeply waiting for the air support. Focusing binoculars
on hands of unsuspecting lovers

who were groping at each other's crotch
sprawled out on the back seat of their Mercury convertible

I didn't see the sniper crouched above us
under outcrop stone until he fired.   The report

was filed away as classified; the mission order was *abort*.

III

Things your mother said from time to time
are all she ever says today forgetting mostly any speech at all
but Georgetown's by the river
picture show e.g. & don't stay out past eight in the ravine & don't go to the swimming pool you'll get exposed to polio he'll take you in the motorcar & shut the blinds and windas good night nurse I'd just as leave I'd just as soon and you out yakin on the davenport asfarasezconcern that record on the gramaphone'll make me nervous as a cat.

We'd go to triple features at the Hudson. *Bwana Devil, House of Wax, The Charge at Feather River*. Objects hurled at us from the screen. Sitting in the dark and wearing Polaroids we didn't think of objects hurling through the sky but all the 52s up there were practicing LeMay's attack on Leningrad by nuking down electric duds on Dayton and Columbus. You go to Hillside House with Alzheimer's and drool. Otherwise you get a window with a view and lots of Xanax.

She tells you she's in Georgetown and at school
says it's spring it's autumn now she knows because her ears are red she says it's nice outside and would you like some lemonade.

See they masturbate like we do with this clitoris right here.

Ned had recently acquired a Kinsey and was pointing at a diagram. Nell would open up her labia and smile. As the congregation sang out *I was glad* the scholars of Westminster exercised their right acclaimed their sovereign shouting *vivat vivat* as she made her way along the choir. She put her golden girdle on & tried the spurs on the Archbishop who presented her the Rod as massed trumpets sounded & as cannon at the Tower fired salutes.

Could you back-breed objects like a race horse hurl a chainjack into Oppenheimer's calculations? Bohr and Heisenberg were only made of observations on the day we took down all the orbiting electrons from the model and Professor Einstein poured out drinks for Dylan Thomas on a field of praise he'd failed to unify.

That's why Dark Star nosed out Native Dancer in the Derby.

That's why teleology had hidden *De Re Militari* in a cave
and Ethel Rosenberg smiled like Mona Lisa

and the Pumpkin Papers that convicted Alger Hiss
convinced the archaeologists at Khirbet Qumran.

Piltdown jaws away at time gone tipsy as we scar our faces rubbing red clay in our wounds and take our oaths. Beria broke down completely wept and begged them for his life. He'd give them dachas by the sea, he'd give them Stalin's pets and playmates, Lenin's secret penthouse in New York. They dragged him down the corridor and down the stairs and pushed him to his knees against the wall. They shot him with a pistol in the brain.

That's why both her ears are red it's nice outside and would you like some lemonade.

That's why by the outcrop stone one summer night when no moon rose up over the
    ravine
and I was watching *I Love Lucy* or *The Red Skelton Show*
Ned committed incest with his sister

                                                                          or it wasn't why.

IV

He only said he did it and he really didn't.
He didn't really do it but he bet she said he did.
She said he did it but she didn't know he couldn't when he didn't do it and she said.
He said I really did it but she didn't know it.

Then Kikuyu Central spoke up for Kenyatta. We all prayed solemnly to missionary
god Mwathani Ngai but to old Mwene old Nyaga too. We ate the meat of Miss Kirk-
patrick's dachshund and of Mr. Macintosh's cat, pierced the sodom apple & the sheep's
eye with our thorns. They passed a calabash of blood around our shaven heads and we
traded them our foreskins for their cigarettes.

As members of the forest gang we'd hamstring livestock, burn the grain stores, terrify
the Europeans with machetes. Then we heard about the Vietminh and thought we'd
drive the French into the sea. Even so the *Isle de France* had its attractions and we
saved a crew of twenty-six whose freighter sank in mid-Atlantic storms.

No one said you were the Mortgenröthemensch, but I ask you was that jaw Orang-
utang? That year patination of a Van Dyck brown was revealed as potassium-bichro-
mate stain. You wore your piltdown cranium like Uncle Edward's blue beret and
found the hippo bones out in the quarry.

Disasters follow dermatology precede
disciples and discrimination in employment. First up in the Es is Eastern Orthodoxy
but you'd never met the Patriarch in Istanbul and neither he would lay you odds
had Julian schismatics like Chrysostom Cavouridis.

Epikataratos pas ho kremamenos epi xylou.

She walked along the golden carpet toward the royal gallery and Chair of the Estate.
Judges, bishops, officers and peers were in their stalls. They offered her the bread.
They offered her the wine. The congregation sang *All People That On Earth Do
Dwell*. Then they placed the leather strap across her mouth and dropped the hood

and buckled down her arms and wrists and legs. When the current hit her body it appeared as if she tried to stand, her hands shriveled into furious little fists.

In the Abbey everybody cheered. Your mother said your father's right you give them back their cigarettes and don't stay out past eight in the ravine. Take me home she said don't sell the house I can't remember quite which one you are you know I really don't live here I'm only visiting.

And eschatology took Ethel from our alphabet and made Good Friday dance listening to Crusoe on the juke box and with Julius already gone.

He'd pierce the sodom apple & the sheep's eye with his thorn.
He'd hamstring livestock join the Vietminh or meet schismatics for a lemonade.
He'd telephone Kikuyu Central for the Mortgenröthemensch.

We did the executions readily enough, strapping one another down and playing anthems on an old kazoo. Nell preferred to play the queen but she was also good at making little fists & jerking from the hips when hit by say two thousand volts delivered at a full eight amperes.

He said she did it but he didn't know she couldn't when she didn't do it and he said.

V

A little Ritalin a little Prozac or a Zoloft if you please. These Mothers for a Mild Millennium; these Ladies for a Later Lexicon. Telekenetic, though, and Sabbaterian. She says it's like the hoosegow here you know the callaboose the clink the lockup where they send the sinners overdosed on neuroleptics and you'd better come another day.

Beneath the overhang of weeping-willow limbs
propped in wheelchairs beside the quiet waters and decidedly another day—
their voices made of lilac
and their gestures made of hay.

In the summer Ned and Nell were saved. They'd shout and sing. At the Pentecostal Church you'd pass that looked like some abandoned warehouse with a whitewashed cross nailed to a plain black door. She gave up fashion shows and executions and we all gave up the Mau Mau massacres and Khumbu Glacier climbs. They'd met the Mortgenröthemensch and it was them. While I stood listening by a window terrified to go inside they'd sing their cipher out like KGB cryptologists before their time.

They'd speak in languages the slain in spirit know their xenogloss an antiphon to all the glossolalias of man.

That September I returned to school. Everyone seemed all at once to be thirteen. We'd crouch beneath long tables in the cafeteria, hook our arms behind our heads protecting face and neck against the flash. It was a drill. It was the bomb. Somehow we'd survive if we could just protect that tender flesh that burned.

You wondered crouching there how many had been saved. Was Eisenhower saved? Was Syngman Rhee? You hunkered down.

How about Kenyatta and Chrysostom Cavouridis?
The men up there in 52s the men in MIGs the men in missile silos in Ukraine?

Were Ethel at the deli and the Ethel in the Chair and executioner Francel and the
          Essenes?
Tell me Joel about the former rain about the latter rain the later lexicon the prophecy and weeping willows by the quiet waters and the lemonade.

And underneath a table in a cave or overhang of weeping willow limbs or down a glen or in an abbey or an execution chamber someone says you did it when you didn't or you really didn't when you really did and hands you the binoculars a gold ampulla with a little spoon a ticket to *The House of Wax* an orb a sodom apple and a thorn. For-get the foreskins and the cigarettes. And no need for the spectographic studies if you're targeted because you'll only be a shadow on the ruins of a cafeteria wall.

Dawnman was a mensch all right and in this country anything is possible O dim and lonely Piltdown bluff it's great it's Greek to me.

So what's to say at Pentecost if no one wears a satin collar spreads her labia and takes a picture or a Zoloft or an oath or all the orbiting electrons from the model stays out late in the ravine and nails a pork chop to the flagpole in the middle of the camp.

Gloss it from the glossolalia as *epi xylou: qillat ĕlōhîm tālûy*.
Chainjack way down range
a firestorm's megadeath and back-breed in 3-D.

A shirt blown off of someone's back is hanging like a banner in a blasted tree.

Part Four

. . .

I

The year before I'd worked for ninety cents an hour shuffling IBM cards people folded spindled mutilated I suppose it looked as though I sat there playing solitaire I had to earn enough to get somehow to what I called Constantinople what I called Byzantium in spite of all for she had gone to Turkey with her family Cora had. Her file was her father's double A for Architecture Archeology okay.

One long year alone and counting
her anatomy in drifting mind in reverie at work while auditing
those spindlefolded mutilates her architecture

she had offered me when we were seventeen
had placed my hand deliberately on her ass as we stood blinking
at the sidelines in the autumn mist & watched

our classmates gallop on some county football field

never even had you been away from home more than a month or so in Michigan perhaps Wisconsin just some family holiday and now you muttered to yourself beginning yet another box of Aakers Aarons and Abairs about the gold mosaics on a wall about the hammered gold and gold enameling and brought up sharply by Abdallah Joseph Abdel-Rahman Zenebee.

1961 this time. Box and volume index income tax and yearly rebate post or posting or to claim oh Abbett Brenda Abel Betty Abernathy Charles.
Ave or avaunt there Axelrod and Aycock Ayres Ayu Azzarito LJ Babbit a new beat.

His letters home from 1926 this time are somehow boxed with mine from Istanbul he's at the Belview Biltmore Florida and always writes in pencil always says Dear Folks he's someone in these letters that I never knew he's happy having beaten the rheumatic fever having just got up and on his feet I guess he hasn't met my mother yet he's only twenty-one and didn't have to think about
the neurofibrillary tangles in his brain the helicals in pairs the microtubules or
tau proteins phosphorylated beta-amyloids
or chromosome fourteen.

Russians that year orbited the earth. That put everybody on alert in Anatolia including Cor. You gambled all your Betas and abandoned Amy Loid at the Helical way out in Tau betting no one found the gene for chromosome fourteen and paid your way by IBM by audit and by alphabet. And Ernest Hemingway blew out his brains in Idaho.

Between the shuffles of an Axelrod
Telli Babba blessed a virgin on the Bosphorus and physics

blasted nuclei to mason rho and meson pi.
Biochemistry induced the birth of a synthetic RNA.

You wondered if the Hittites took cuneiform from the Assyrians if Phocaeans emigrated west if Pax Romana could dissolve in olive oil and wine and could you get there on the Gnostic airlines before June
if Constantine intended first of all to rebuild Troy.

II

All so long ago it seems hallucinated now. Eighteen. And walking by the Black Sea with your suicidal love. Your letters home a tourist's recitation or resuscitation not to be resisted in recitative. Her body your obsession and your pockets full of condoms spilling in their silver wrappers in the sand.
Rhapsodists rewired then with rhenium for rhyme.
It wasn't Florida in 1926 dear folks.

Elsewhere it is always midnight always Maidenek and Belsen. Transportation officers subordinate he says Servatius arguing against the jurisdiction of the court. The man himself behind his glass and taking notes in pencil on a little pad. A tool in the hands of a malignant fate he says. Abducted from the Argentine. Malignant fate a tool. His hands malignant as his fate. His tool in his hands.

Hotel. Oh tell O'Tool.
In what far lands against what falling evil. And in what mirror in what twisting corridor you'd find this Amy Loid this chromosome fourteen and not remember any more. You'd wear a Fez you'd finger strings of little beads you could

right now drive past her house by making just a tiny detour on the way back to the nursing home. The architect her father's still alive. She herself you haven't seen for almost thirty years. And would you recognize her now. And would she know the graybeard sitting in his car and staring stupidly at her front door. Everything as strange just down the road as down the years. Hotel. Oh tell. Her legs spread open there but ah her lips astounding you with I must tell you that while you've been gazing moonily

upon my yearbook picture for three thousand years I've had so many men you couldn't
count them all.

You'd count them all. There's Ajax Agamemnon and Achilles and there's Atatürk
and General Yassiada Nazim Hikmet Yuri A Gagarin Sultan Abdul Hamid and his
seven sons John Foster Dulles and Makarios of Cyprus all of them successful down
the road or down the years although it must be said that Gary Cooper
Ty Cobb Dashiell Hammett
Carl Gustav Jung Dag Hammarskjöld Sam Rayburn Eero Saarinen
and Ernest Hemingway (already mentioned) died.

Onomastics no has nothing in the world to do
with Onan son of Judah or the onager a stone-propelling engine
of the siege the wild ass of central Asia no it's just

a listing of the folks a kind of wedding invitation
or a seating plan the order of an execution
it's a catalogue of ships. I'm really loving this amazing summer

here upon the plains of Anatolia near the winedark sea.
So what if she has had this little thing with Abdul Hamid
and the boys oh and yes the other little things

(fill in at will the names provided on your list).
It's me she really loves. The postcard shows
you Hisarlik where Heinrich Schliemann dug up Troy.

That's me beside the gallows where they hung Menderes in July.
The transportation officer is on the right.

III

Displacement of the *c* and *h* invests the *gens* and so it's
Eigen isn't Eich or Manicore if vertebrate is shown

he may inherit in his haunted house regressive genes
more readily if organisms crave their transportation

into cave the better to survive in Konya you could ruminate
on Rumi like a troglodite

rummy or canasta was
the game she played the game you see them playing still up on the second floor in
wheel chairs their minds still there still focused on the playing cards whose own dear
folks had not transported chromosome fourteen.

Dear Folks: We took the ferry from the European to the Asian side in only twenty
minutes; then we sailed down the coast. They brought us tea in little glasses as the sky
line full of minarets began to fade. Efendi stood up by the rail shouting *spaka gimek*.
Literally that means put on a hat. Shoes on feet and pants on legs a shirt and tie a
jacket and a waistcoat that's what old Mustafa Kemel said he said whereas

in rummy or canasta you must meld. It's not the same in Rumi. Sequence has no value
suits no meaning here. You hope for jokers and red threes. It's runic as can be among
these Anglo-Saxons of the second floor but would you play it on your melophone and
could you find a mandate in Koranic law?

He says at the conclusion—he is twenty-one, it's 1926—that he would rather not
come home would rather not go on to law school disappointing news he understands
but that is how he feels. He hopes he says in some mysterious way to make his family
proud of him he says he hasn't taken any medicine at all these past three months he
feels confident he says he's happy now and he was I would say a miserable man for his
entire life he came back home he studied law he married Lois K out there where she
inherits in her haunted house I visit her again I write it down.

That year retranslated Paul to the Ephesians retranslated John while summer gaucho
Klement alias the abductee the man expert in sealed trains listened with his ear-
phones looking darkly through his glass. They'd take you to the Aesculapium where
it was written only death forbidden here and down into the tunnels down into the
basement temple where a priest of Pergamum would whisper through the speaking
tube be well be well

they drugged the hopeless cases absolutely dotty everybody
thought they heard the voice of a god

or at Nicaea or in 325.
Constantine held every joker every last red three.
Spaka gimek. Go put on a hat

in that hotel. Or walking by the winedark sea.
And swimming out in it—

Swimming out so far I thought she'd drown
I thought the only thing she wanted

was to die.

IV

Her father's job was reassembling temples. Expert also in the Esperanto of assorted eschatologists and an impediment to your desires he answered when the pedocals of arid regions called and was a pedagogue whose pebbles were on offer to Pelagians. We helped him dig and sift and sort.

It would have been a pagan holiday
all Roman baths and pornographic movies at the theatre

except for Paul & John & the apocalyptic angel
seven stars in his right hand & walking in the midst of all the archaeologists

the dervish dancing where sweet Artemis once dwelled
a reed plucked from her marsh a flute

bewailing separation from her bed of reeds

while at the nursing home they opened up the seventh seal. Then she turned and in the moonlight by the temple gate undid her bodice looking at you frankly and you saw at once the heaving of her twenty breasts pearled in the tiny drops of a lactescent dew. But if you harbor chromosome fourteen the time will come when you remember none of this. Take me home she says don't sell the house I don't remember quite which one you are you know I don't live here I'm only visiting.

Canasta decks cascading to the floor. The sound of distant castanets.

Dear folks: we disembarked at Port Coressus then passed through the Harbor Gate and walked the length of marble pavement lined with colonnades and shops until we reached the tetraphylon like the one you know in Palestine. Once they isolated lepers as you will recall but now it is the old like you who must be swept from the agora off beyond the gate of Mithradates where we shut them up in colonies as if old age itself were a contagion and they shuffle down the hallways on their walkers sometimes lashing out with canes. One old geezer Erosthostenes has said he knows a way to enter history

to claim immortal fame he'll burn Diana's temple
down where after Ephesus the Es on offer
will include the epicycle and the epidemic and the epilogue

epiphany a feast on January 6 and Erebus a state of mind
resistant to epistemology the epsilon
equivocal but there on your escutcheon anyway

and so that's me again beside Effendi in my Fez. Heinrich Schliemann on my left and
on my right the hangman and the judge. In Washington Casals is playing Allemandes
for JFK in Upper Arlington the ladies on the second floor are playing cards. My father
is in Florida it's 1926. No one drowns herself in that year's southern sea. Effendi tells me
go put on a hat. I said in what hotel. I said not Onan son of Judah nor the onager.

Everybody on alert all over Anatolia.
Hotel. Or tell which temple eschatology rebuilds.

Which are you the epidemic or the epilogue. Oh epsilon my son!
45326 acknowledges his number in his glass.

V

Your story then. That too in the box. You called her Margaret there and you yourself
were Richard but not here. Your Istanbul looks more like Alexandria than Istanbul.
Doubtless you were reading Lawrence Durrell who was hot in 1961. When the crazy
family and the randy lover of the eldest daughter get out to the ruins everything im-
plodes. But Margaret doesn't try to drown herself in any sea. Hotel. I tell her father
you can call me epsilon. He says I'll call you Otto Ottoman I'll call you Byzantine Bill.
I say they say your daughter's fucking Abdul Hamid and his seven sons. He says we
disembarked at Port Coressus then passed through the Harbor Gate and walked the
length of marble pavement lined with colonnades and shops until we reached the tet-
raphylon like the one you know in Palestine. He says they'd take you to the Aescu-
lapium where it was written only death forbidden here and down into the tunnels
down into the basement temple where a priest of Pergamum would whisper through
the speaking tube be well be well

beware dear folks of eschatology he says the millineries
and their hats the radar
gazing at a millenary sky. She says Hotel. I know it's a hotel. I tell them
that I don't live here I tell them how

77

the rummy players meld
and how the transportation officer explains The Way. Tau proteins
form a halo around senile plaques.
He hopes to make his family proud of him he hasn't taken any medicine at all.

That was Cora and not Margaret swimming out to sea.

Your story then. A shuffle only in the IBMs detaches all the Aakers from the Abdel-Rahman Zenebees. A shuffle only when you try to walk. Hotel. A temple bell. A reed plucked from her marsh a flute bewailing separation from her bed of reeds. You took the ferry from the European to the Asian side and then sailed down the coast. They brought in tea in little glasses as the sky line full of minarets began to fade. Effendi stood up by the rail shouting *spaka gimek*. Also Ephesus. Also SOS. And when she turned there by the temple she undid her bodice looking at you frankly and you saw at once the heaving of her twenty breasts. In that hotel. Her legs spread open there her lips astounding you with such bad news. You wondered if the Hittites took cuneiform from the Assyrians. You'd wear a fez. You'd finger strings of little beads although they didn't do it this way in Ohio.

At Catal Hüyük some 4000 years before Egyptian pyramids Diana's chthonic shape appears in figurines uncovered in the neolithic hills. Not far from Hisarlik. Not far from Upper Arlington where you drove slowly past her house those nights of playing Scrounge with Joel and Carl. She'd be there, all right, standing in her shorts and bathed entirely in yellow light. Your story then. You won't be overlooked by the geneticist.

You empty out the boxes one and one by one
your letters and your father's and your fictions

where you cower in the future's flame
as works and days unnumber and you do forget

well almost all of it the whole damn thing
gone blank in time and you too in the cards

with Zoetrope and Zero and the Zenebees.

Part Five

. . .

I

I think I heard him saying *and he still drinks alcohol*
and laughing like he'd said I still drank Kool Aid.
He himself of course "took drugs."
Three of us were pissing on a walnut tree.

That was I suppose at Jim Black's place up in Los Altos hills the year when Al Guerard
had tried to woo back west a scowling Irving Howe by taking him to what he'd hoped
would be sufficiently outrageous student parties. *Dissent's Gone Soft On The Imperialists*
proclaimed a banner hanging up above the band. But on the other hand.

Urinalysis of schizophrenics shows a trace of something like
Methoxyphenylethylamine.
Bump off every single nitrogen and your compounding chemist
grinds you up the flowering tops of those deflowered female hemps:
Tetrahydrocannabinol.

Polysyllables for Sixty-Six and you yourself polygamous almost. Polyphonic anyway
and polytheistic. Powers of attorney put you in another's hands: & to perform which
act and acts what thing and things whatever the device and the devices in the law
whatever may be needful necessary in my name to do to execute and to perform it
largely amply and to all intents and purposes as I might do if I were present and per-
forming it myself
shall never be
affected by my disability my incapacity
incompetence or lapse of time.

Two of us had lapsed into a corner of the time where coffee was the thing at two a.m.
We show each other poems. One of us is to become the Poet Laureate. Not me. Poet
Laureate of the United States. Your sickly father was alive and came out to your wed-
ding. Your mother was quite fit and had no need to give up any power. Your friend
would marry you okay but did not love you welladay. This was 1966. This was swim-
ming in the Yangtze and a US H-bomb missing in the sea near Palomares. This was
the Miranda case and anybody's right to stand up silently. This was mining harbors in
Haiphong apartheid in South Africa and Lin Piao on culture. This was avalanche in
Rio and a BOAC jet exploding at the foot of Fuji. Claiming your Miranda rights
you'd stand up silently when asked

does anybody know a reason why this woman and this man

should not abide in Methoxyphenylethylamine
as long as they both shall live?

Your father would not now live long.
What's left of him I've packed up in a box with all his yearbooks.

All the books of all those years I've numbered here
to parse out features in a body of the past that took its measures

all dissent gone soft on the Imperialists
laughing like you drank some Kool Aid

lapsed into the corner of a time.

II

Most of magic in the drug you hoped they took was in the pill they called the pill the period coming on like clockwork every month and no more need for condoms or to come in someone's open hands I loved it in the shower when she'd bend down with her wet hair on my thighs and with her mouth almost although the one you marry on inspired impulse may decide within a year you will not do you kept it up with two or three you knew before her time you'd grieve when she went off with R who knew more than the rest of us about the war who'd been in combat in Korea no one could believe he was that old.

God the druggist staring at me when I started in with Cora and would have to ask for Trojan-enz with maybe who could tell some colleague of my father's in the line behind me or the cousin older sister aunt of someone in my class
and then you'd have to specify the lubricated kind and he'd pretend he hadn't heard and you at fifty-five remember this and impotent sometimes.

Beta blockers digitalis and its glycosides diazepam and half the stuff
you're on impair erections

even diuretics and the TAD's. And then he asked me if I still drank alcohol.
Mao and Lin Piao could tell you power was the real

aphrodisiac. But how much should you take and how long should you take it and do benefits outweigh the risks?

Do I need to take any special precautions? Are there side effects
I should expect?

She tries to phone the street address and then sends off a letter to the telephone:
Martha Jane and Mary Kay at Hudson 43402. She cannot understand the nurse who
cannot understand her patient when she says go get that man who fixes Gramaphones.
I put the yearbooks in a cardboard box. I do it largely amply and to all intents and
purposes as she might do it were she present and performing this herself
in San Francisco by the Longshoreman's Hall.
And just like any tourist in the Day-Glo silent night whose Dada metamorphosis
could suffer an arrest and call it love.

That year Maoists starved their neurons and deprived their
neurofilaments of dopamine. Then they ran
like Mau Maus through Peking. Power was the proposition

power was the drug. And as I write that down
I hear a boom-box in the street I hear a voice that's disembodied
keening elegy for Captain Trips.

In San Francisco by the Longshoremen's Hall not a single cadre dressed like peasants
no one dragged the mayor from his bed or burned his books or smashed his tablets in
the public square. You starved your neurons and deprived your neurofilaments of
dopamine by other means. Why not be a literalist of the imagination why not say the
people's opium is opium. You did. Your dead. You dithered there. Bore fraternal
greetings to the Chief of State to Liu Shao-chi to party General Secretary Teng Hsiao-
ping and begged them not to follow in the line that wound up from the Wharf and to
the cinema where everybody waited for Zhivago in the dark and listened for the bal-
alaika like a broken like a balabalabalalaika.

III

R had "occupied" the office of the president with several friends from SDS. Now he's
occupied as president himself. They sat around the office drinking beer. We ourselves
by then "took drugs." Three of them were pissing on the walnut desk, dissent gone
soft on the Imperialists. Feet up on the gleaming surface, cigarettes stubbed out in
presidential tray, R concerned himself with dials that would amplify the Dylan songs
on out the window and across the quad. And in an early poem the Laureate's red eye

flashed from Palo Alto "clean as malice" through the fog in Redwood City where they made the napalm by the bay. He thought, he said, about the village of Bien Hoa

so did you a little bit
and went to live in London out in Islington.

The nurse was fired who took her Demoral.
The Beatles were more popular than Jesus.

I suppose it's possible Akhmatova had died
the very moment Yuri first saw Lara as that movie

ran in London Paris San Francisco
& the paper opened up in someone's hands

across the isle you were in the train the Circle line you watched the movie thinking back on Sister Life you had not been as you had thought you'd be the future's guest in someone's Poem Without a Hero but you overhear the nurse who jabbers on just like your students saying *so I'm like and then he goes*

what was she like where did he go
that year that swallowed up Akhmatova Jean Arp André Breton Montgomery Clift & Buster Keaton Hedda Hopper Admiral Chester Nimitz Giacometti Frank O'Connor Disney. Married just six months and now the ocean for a fact between us R had shown me that book *Ariel* and asked me *Do you have a rubber crotch?*

97,000 there in Wembley and when Geoffrey Hurst kicks in the winning goal the country goes completely nuts even Harold Wilson and the Queen. 400,000,000 watch this on TV. The World Cup's elixir or a hemlock Dear you look so tired today. Franglais entered dictionaries. Aleotoric big bang theory camp.

REM and screen pass po-faced mini eldercare.
The Frug. The Hype.
Go-go jump-cut bonkers. Royal Shakespeare does the persecution of Marat performed by inmates of the Charenton asylum as directed by De Sade and Dr. Freidenberg. Mentation better once she went off Haldol and the Prozac back in February still she's in decline Language is aphasic Manifests agnosia and paranoia lately Gait is shaky and she'll need a cane. You'll notice frequently the verbal paraphasias. Word substitutions. DAT.

He reads the REMs hooks up electrodes

and determines which dementias can be classified AT.

Why not first unzip the rubber crotch.

Is that an evil eye my love or something newly alloy a prosthetic made of plastics
or a part that resurrects.

How does Komsomol serve Communism. Translate and provide your gloss.

IV

There you sat where Karl Marx once sat and wrote your London poems. All about divorce. You might have known you'd only manage such a theme even having come so far for revolution. Sit there long enough and maybe echoes from the roundhouse walls would penetrate. You couldn't concentrate. You smoked and drank. Fifteen minutes in the reading room and then an hour's break across the street with Players and a pint. Echoes from the roundhouse walls
as you continue down the halls with plastic garbage bags.

A certificate that he attained the 33rd degree. Supreme court robe. Campaign buttons all the way from Harrison and Grant. A drawer entirely full of corks. Another full of soy sauce containers. Plastic compact in a bathroom cabinet there among the decades old prescriptions and you lift it open with a finger nail in surprise behold

her diaphragm. Diabolic how they'll give you diacetylmorphine for just a simple case of diachronics. Diagnosis at some weird diagonal to diakinesis. You sat there at your desk to diagram the dialectic but regretted you had never danced the old diaspora before Diaghilev completed his dialysis.

Nurses wheel their patients in and run the film. On a screen the size of Mt. Olympus geriatric porn queens lick each other's cunts. An imagery the Laureate declared in his first book consisting like America in lack of scale. Back there in the distance is Zhivago trudging through the snow. He's on the scent. Up ahead are Lara Beatrice Penelope and Cor. Mao had virgins brought in by the dozen, never took a bath, wouldn't brush his teeth. For months on end did not get out of bed. Take me home she said don't sell the house I can't remember quite which one you are you know I really don't live here I'm only visiting. Let him without sinanthropus cast the first Red Guard

and arm him with this closet full of swords.

Enough indeed to start a fencing school if in need of uniforms for everyone you empty six or seven wards. Edward's unstrung cello back there in the dark, a stack of

primers to initiate the rites on some Masonic stage. They gave you numbers in the
reading room. You spoke your part as if you were enraged
engaged on every front at once imagine dear your mind become so like a boil
did you wind the spring of your electric heart.

When does too much of imagine dear become disease.
When does mind become a boil that must lance itself.

Sinanthropus did manage to stand up erect
achieved the use of fire and certain tools for example crudely fashioned axe
for example twenty kiloton device exfoliating near Lob Nor he was
discovered circa 1929 at Choukoutien it is not thought
he understood the red shift of Quasars but he lifted up his eyes
but he beheld the sky.

Homology. Homophony. Homeric Hymn.

March northeast to Honan province and display her diaphragm your diagram
of all electric circuits at the San Men project
or your relics of the stone age at the San Men gorge. Mercy mercy

Madame Mao he'd call out Mother of us all I'd call out mine.

V

The phenomenology of anti-fascist pharmacologists.
The flower in the flame.
The lama whose La Mancha was Lamarckian.

And Mary Quant that year was made an OBE for introducing miniskirts where fash-
ion plates had illustrated farthingales. You fell in love. Again. Against your better
judgment. Judging from disasters in your past. You'd pass on tricks conditioned by
this new environment. No pasquinade that year all pas de deux where party line dis-
solved in passacaglia the proteins never flowing the right way. Nonetheless had T.
Lshenko risen in the great red dawn to celebrate inherited callosities among the mid-
wife toads and many men who since have chosen Cavorject.
Simply self-inject the penis and the medicine will go to work.
Only half of one percent develop Priapism but if you're unlucky, brother, plan to
spend the next three days looking like a randy faun upon a Grecian urn.

84

When pharmacologists compounded their phenomena, Omega dreamed. Alpha held
the hands of her ontologist. Pasturage extended out from Islington to Aldeburgh and
you grazed a while in pastoral relief. Tupping in your tuppence worth of mental as-
troturf you muttered your tu quoque through a proxy in the courts

divorce become an art of divination
in a phase of every trial called discovery.

Aphasia then. And ever afterwards in Asia
world without any end amend.

Printed as required by the Scientologists.

I ask them how much she remembers how much she can understand this execution
which on her behalf releases other documents consents to this Do Not Resuscitate this
paper that prohibits interventions that prohibits both nutrition and hydration but al-
lows whatever drugs may be obtained to kill the pain ontology a function of oncology if

protein synthesis and polymeric vectors
mean you are your mother's son your father's fated cowboy
polypeptides flowing like the war

of generations information only out of the nucleic acids Pavlov buried
in a Skinner box with all the roots
of real numbers in a digit that's both decimal and arbitrary.

Tower bridge Falangists drew their falchions if you fell in with the Trotskyites your
politics as puny as falsetto false arrest the agent of her living will the ticket for Tbilisi
in your pocket and Manuel de Falla blazing at the Proms in Albert Hall.

From Abyssinia to ablative the dosage
is discovered by the dice the delitescent absolute beyond the will

the year run down the tide run out at Tilbury.
She says so Illbeseeinya ram beau   she says

do not resuscitate   do not   let go

Cuttings

sail archangel agrimony avens
broom & burdock

eyebright fumitory meadow sweet
so the mountain flax & mugwort so the sanicle

and all indigenous medicinals be meet

elsewhere also sail & what's the use
& where's the hemlock woodsage yarrow find

some bird of paradise

& what's archangel agrimony avens to
strelitzia reginae

la triomphe royale la majestieuse

cuttings & endeavors & a mezzotint
record a bank & there the wild thyme blows

& oxlips & the nodding violet grows

I

Five Cuttings with Endeavors
& Repeated Incantation

1 John Tradescant

Robert Cecil's man became the Duke of Buckingham's
became the King's. Dudley Digges took
him to Archangel.
Later the Algerians who followed
Barbarossa led him to the lilac and narcissus fields
and granted him a vision of the coming
of the sons of Joseph Banks.

What land was promised? What pomp
would suit their circumstances when they brought
the seeds and seedlings for the King?

*

O Bird of Paradise—Strelitzia Reginae, Lord!—
Chincherinchee. Chincherinchee.
Ixia viridiflora! Ixia cinnamomea, too!

Endeavors

The transit of Venus. Tupia. The love
of nut-brown maids. They'd reached Tahiti
and begun to feed on bread-plants.
All of them a-tupping went
except for Parkinson, the Quaker
with the keen eye and the cautious morals.
Specimens were pressed between
the proof sheets of a job lot ream of Addison—
his commentary on *Paradise Lost*.
Banks gave all the chiefs the names he thought
would suit them—Ajax, Hercules, Lycurgus.
In his journal, Parkinson complained
that Mr. *Monks and Mr. Banks*
came to an éclaircissement and nearly dueled.
All for favors of Othea Thea.
Of Tupia, Banks told Captain Cook—*I'll keep*
him as a curiosity like neighbors
back in England keep their lions.

Venus made her transit. Officially observed.
Mr. Green packed up his quadrant
and the botanists their specimens and
watercolors of the flora, fish, and dancing girls,
the shoreline profiles & the long canoes.
A month surveying Huahine, Tahaa, Raiatea
left them open sea and just a crescent
on the Tasman chart of 1642 that might be
Tara Australis and landfall or might not.
Banks made inventory of the sheep and fowls,
the south sea hogs, the boar & sow & litter,
bins of sauerkraut to stave off scurvy.
In his journal Parkinson observed the
water within reefs . . . *seagreen breakers white*
in many bays all stript & streakt with purple
by an intervention of the cloud between
the sun and surface . . . cat's paws if a wind
comes up on swells & it is calm . . .
Sea so like some foreign thing in flower.

2 Francis Masson

The Hottentots had fallen in the hippo pools
and Francis Masson, botanizing out of Cape Town
on his way to river Olyfont, wrote it in his diary.
Also this: *I myself have nearly drowned.*

The African geranium would find its way to Yorkshire—
the tritonias, gladioli, & the ancestors of bulbs
that Mrs. Boden-Smith planted in her window box last fall.
Boers supplied the the cannabis. He'd forded Duvvenhoek

and headed for the hills in pouring rain.

*

Mesembryanthemum.
Crassula and cotyledon and
euphorbia!
          Euphoria had seized him

as he found them all along the Little Cape Karoo known
as Canaan's Land. Then came collywobbles
from a collop of bad beef he'd barbecued.
Mum was the word
as he crossed Van Stadaaens,
noting in his diary the vast and grazing herds
of buffalo.

Endeavors

Fifty-seven days they climbed the swells
heaving in from West South West.
Pintados passed, an albatross. Eventually
a sailor spotted seaweed clinging to
a piece of wood. Cook observed two seals.
Twice, a morning fogbank brought
the shout of land; then they saw New Zealand.

Everything was strange: hostile Maoris with
their curling black tattoos who ate
their captives boiled in a pot with dogs;
forget-me-nots with leaves the size
of rhubarb; arborescent lilies; daisies growing
to the height of trees. . . .

           Tupia, who
got the gist of native speech, explained
that Maoris who appeared in a canoe
were selling those four severed heads
they held up by the hair. Banks
arranged a trade for one—they took some
iron and beads—and put it
in his sea chest wrapped in flax.

3 Allan Cunningham

And Allan Cunningham wrote at once
to Kew: *we put in at the south shore*
of Endeavour —just where you yourself & Cook
first came. . . .
                    We too were attacked—with spears
and clubs and boomerangs—but managed to fight off
the Aboriginals with musketry.

How much pleasure we derived in tracing your own steps
and those of Dr. Solander, finding on the
surface and the muddy shaded edge of lowland ponds
the ornamental Melastoma banksii. . . .

        *

Australia. The Melastoma named for Banks himself,
the river for the ship of Captain Cook.

They found the ruined *Frederick*, washed up on
the rocks a year before. They found
a pile of coal collected on the beach by Banks'

own men. It kept them warm through one cold night.
Meanwhile, off the archipelago called
Buccaneer for William Dampier the pirate,

corals grew and twisted
with the patience of an anthozoan's dream time.

Endeavors

Flax and pine would one day mark endeavors
of another kind—Pitt's advisors measuring
the hawsers, canvas, sailcloth and cordage
in their minds, staring up at the imagined pines
that rose a hundred feet in forests full of
mainmasts, spars and jib booms where they'd
spread the sails that would rule the waves.
New Zealand flax; Norfolk Island pine.
And some armed haven not far off where soldiers
could protect refitting ships and where, perhaps,
transplanted felons might take root and bloom.

All these London musings ten years off as Banks
wrapped up his severed Maori head
and Cook, beyond the trade winds, sailed west
hoping for a landfall indicated by the scrap
on Tasman's chart. South winds drove him northward
and in April Parkinson could draw the mouth
of what they first called Sting Ray Bay
and later Botany. . . .

4 *Robert Fortune*

He'd shaved his head and made
himself a pigtail, passing as Chinese at Shoo-chow-foo.
Not a single local called him *Kwei-tsz*—
Child of a foreign devil out for trade.

His instructions had been plain:
Find the two-pound peaches of Pekin.
Find the place where *Enkianthus* shrubs grow wild.
Find the double yellow rose
the plant to make rice paper
all bamboos of every kind the lilies
Chinese eat like boiled chestnuts
bright blue peonies
azaleas from Ho-fou-shau.

                    *

He hadn't known about Jan-dous who
tried to board his junk while sailing to Chu-shan,
but nonetheless he blew the helmsman off the stern
with just one pistol shot and left
the pirate ship with flapping sails.
He'd bring *Anemone japonica* to Chiswick—
make it flower better than on ramparts of Shanghai.

                    *

In his luggage—
stones from two enormous peaches
Enkianthus shrubs
bamboos lilies peonies azaleas and one
thin pigtail he'd cut off
when boarding ship at last for home.

Endeavors

Parkinson drew more:—

giant heaths, acacias, flame trees, firs &
honeysuckles, amaryllis, lilies, yellow fronds of wattle,
bright waratah, eucalyptus, scarlet stamens of
the callistemons, grass blades rising up to fourteen feet—
then the frantic cockatoos and parrots flying
all around and calling out, the bear-like wombats
peering from their holes. . . . Banks rowed in to shore
with stacks of drying paper
that he'd quire and spread on sails
in the morning sun.

Cut and save, he'd cut and dry and save.
Everything must get intact to Kew—
fern leaves equally with wallabies and
severed heads and most especially Tupia himself,
his savage prince; he'd take that kangaroo the sailor shot
to London taxidermists, then go lug it off
to Mr. Stubbs who'd hang it from a meat hook,
who'd paint it like a horse. Pull up all the
green things by the roots, draw and quarter, touch
and smell and dry, press
all things of colour into quires & look for more.

5 Richard Spruce

He was a man for mosses and the liverworts.
The sedge he found—*Carex Paradoxa*—had been
walked all over by the English for a thousand years.
But he would name the thing. He'd let them know
the lowly flora would no longer be anonymous

      *

If asked to leave, he'd go—
A man for Yurimaguas when he got the chance.
And for the English he'd describe
enormous trees crawling with fantastic parasites
& hung all over with lianas python-like
and twisted with the fine regularity of cable.
Grasses were bamboos of sixty feet.
Violets the size of apple trees.

      *

Yellow psittacanthi flowers made
the pampas smell like honeysuckle after rain.
A man for the chinchona seeds and barks,
he'd grind the powders for malaria and
send his trees beyond the taint of any Popery
to India or else Sri Lanka. A man
in his canoe well up the Bombanaza in the Andes,
he met the local governor at Paca-Yacu.
No, he said, his name
was not Pizarro the Conquistador.

Guayaquil: he came there with a hundred thousand seeds.

Endeavors

Those impressed by these endeavors choired elsewhere
at the given sign and Englishmen returned
to New South Wales with craftsmen, surgeon, chaplain & marines—
with convicts gazing from the decks of *Sirius*
as captain Arthur Phillip anchored in the bay.

The leadsman had sung Cook & Banks beyond the reef
but half the crew then died of tertian fever in Batavia
and no one ever made a mast of Norfolk Island pine
or mainsails of New Zealand flax.

Died Tupia
Tayeto Monkhouse
Reynolds Corporal Truelove
Parkinson & Green
Died Moody
Haite
Thompson Jordon Nicholson & Woolf.

As Banks and Cook sailed on with specimens
and souvenirs, the Aboriginal *Goodriddance*
spelled its fond farewell more crudely
than the Latin of Linnaeus:
Vale vir sine pare: O Farewell unequaled man.

They threw their excrement at the *Endeavour*'s wake.

    *

O Bird of Paradise—Strelitzia Reginae, Lord!—
Chincherinchee. Chincherinchee.
Ixia viridiflora! Ixia cinnamomea, too!

II

As Kew As You

Francis Masson in Karroo and climbing Bokkeveld
to find the *aloe dichotoma* (Dutchman's Koker Boom) of which
the Hottentots (he notes it in his diary) make quivers—
and old Mr. Frame the famous footpad still out in the sun
to take his beer at Kew whose gang might top a Florizel
outside the Drury Lane but let a thousand flowers bloom
along the green. Came Mr. David Nelson home that year
with news of Cook's dead jackknife in Hawaiian surf
came *Winter's Tale* in summer and young Perdita
the actress Mrs. Mary Robinson to fuck the Prince of Wales
for twenty thousand pounds. Lord Malden waved a handkerchief
to light the inn situated then out on the ait at Brentford.
William Aiton took the pleasure ground and measured it
for madness. Fanny Burney would attend the Queen.

Well before that measure pleasured well the footpad Frame
well both Perdita & Florizel a thousand flowers blooming there
when Cook still sailed and *aloe dichotoma* hid in Bokkeveld
the Hottentots made quivers and the consort patiently awaited
her *Strelitzia* her pretty bird of paradise and Albion especially
all the daughters fair of that same isle Professor Martyn's book:
they'd see he'd say at all times study nature & the taste of frivolous
amusements will abate it shall prevent the tumult & the passion
shall provide the mind with nourishments & all things salutary
filling it with noble objects worthy of its contemplation summer's
winter's tale will nonetheless be told dead jackknife Cook
come home a corpse the heir apparent flash a swollen stamen
from behind Lord Malden's handkerchief in androecium
and Fanny Burney to attend the scene... The Queen that is

no harlot nay née Charlotte Sophia of Mecklenburg-Strelitz
whose drawing-master Francis Bauer taught the ladies of
the court their parts said tip it rarely that ellipse in selfsame plane
with floret rays concavity available through all degrees
until the horizontal when your form is discoid then convex:
repeat it carpel carpellate & column innocent enough but gynoecium
with pistil pencil in and paint. Alarmed past all expression
she ran straight off with all her might but then her terror was to hear
herself pursued to hear the croaking voice of the King himself
all loud & hoarse and calling after her Miss Burney all she knew
was that the orders were to keep out of his way the garden full
of little labyrinths by which she might escape the taste of
frivolous amusements will abate it shall prevent the tumult
passion & provide for Mr. Frame the footpad in the summer sun.

No statue of Aspacia or Asoka there to hide behind she looked
askance aslant the sleeping Frame askew at such asperity
and asked him sir which herbals would be hermeneutic which ellipse
of rays medicinal although you wouldn't physically consume
an illustration of the aster for astasia. Astarte then. Austere the stare
of Reverend Mason his epistle to Sir William Chambers verses
versus Capability he'd seen untutor'd Brown destroy those wonders
from his melon ground the peasant slave had rudely rushed and
level'd Merlin's Cave knocked down the waxen wizard seized
his wand transformed to lawns what late was fairy land & marred
with impious hand each sweet design where Fanny Burney ran and
floret rays turned up at all degrees until the horizontal where the forms
became all discoid then convex the ladies sang out carpel carpellate
and column drank their gin and peered at one another's gynoecium.

West Indian planters' slaves consumed their weight in plantains why
not breadfruits from Tahiti why not send out Bligh once more
for bounty send out one more poor landlubbing botanist from Kew
to pot those plants and float a greenhouse-full some thousand miles
if convicts trod down cotyledons off in Banks' own bay conviction
had it Empire might be served by Spain's merinos bleating there by Hove
returning via Cape Town from Bombay where Francis Masson doubtless
would pass on some seed some sample of his findings old John Smeaton's
pumping engine working with an Archimedes screw some twenty-four feet
long and turned by plodding horses irrigated white house garden nicely
raising fifteen hundred hogsheads in an hour he said she said he heard
somebody say and read on in her book how there beside the Thames
sat all enthroned in vegetative pride to whom obedient sails from realms
unfurrowed brought the unnamed progeny of which she thought.

They'd name that progeny and paint it in their books who rubbed
their pates with salad oil and chased away the rooks instructing
royal nymphs fair as the Oread race who trod Europa's brink to snatch
from wreck of time each fleeting grace. Said Mr. Bauer there's not a plant
at Kew has not been drawn by you or someone of your household with
a skill reflecting on your personage but still I humbly beg you to observe
a tendency to slight the curve in stems misrepresent in leaves the midrib
where the veins must spring commit an error in perspective due to inattention
place the primrose polyanthus oxlip all of those so elementary forms right
down upon their peduncles with dislocated necks prolong a bit the stalk
or axis through the flower to the center whence the petals or divisions
may be made to radiate correctly & beyond a doubt she saw merinos that
the king had bred with convicts copulating in a bed of hyacinths
somewhere it was in lines inebriate divines had drawn or written there

or in that muck composed by Chatterton or Stephen Duck: Kew!
a happy subject for a lengthened lay though thousands write
there's something more to say thy garden's elegance thy owner's state
the highest in the present list of fate O Kew thou darling of the
tuneful nine thou eating house of verse where poets dine she drew
as best she could when Bauer asked her to respect the flower's arts
upon dissection note the size of stamens if betwixt or opposite corolla
parts and draw a line from base of filament to cleft and not regard
as trifling equanimity achieved by deftly gazing long at dried labellum
sepal stalk & style he cried for every flower blooming millions you
will understand have died a turretted and loopholed folly will be built
this very year when Captain Flinders sails out with orders straight
from Banks again to New South Wales he'll take my brother Ferdinand
along to draw those plants and animals Sir Joseph never saw.

Ah what invention graced the strain well might the laureate bard
be vain in praise of Masson in Karoo Professor Martyn's book on Kew
whose groves however misapplied to serve a prince's lust and pride
were by the Monarch's care designed a place of pleasure for the mind
they sang together every one who came to view that progeny sent back
to Kew from realms unfurrowed as the poet wrote on every sort of
frigate still afloat and Bauer took them one by one like maidens who
had been undone and spread their perianths apart to draw with all the
art he'd teach the daughters of the queen who gazed upon such colours
none of them had seen. Delineations of exotic plants and illustrations
orchidaceous taught a zygomorphic flowering flamboyant forms that
only had a precedent in certain iris norms in drawing monkey lizard bee
or spider orchid try to see the shape that looks familiar it's no jape
to say go draw a zygomorph as if it were a vegetating ape. . . .

As Kew as you he heard somebody say who hid behind a bush upon
a lawn where late untutored Brown had rudely rushed and levelled
Merlin's Cave knocked down the waxen wizard seized his wand
Aspacia nor Asoka ever looked upon. As Kew as you repeated many times
the king and consort poets and divines a drawing master Perdita
the Prince of Wales those friends of Mr. Frame still languishing in jails
and those just back from Cape Town or Bombay as Kew as you
the hours that every day the sundials clocked along the garden walk
where Fanny Burney liked to sit and talk or write down in her book
as Kew as you would caw the captain's rook advancing on a bishop
over board at sea en route to bring back yet more loot and plants named
for the Englishmen who sought them out as Kew as you for botanists
to tout & draw transplant dissect in all the ways Sir Joseph would direct
as Kew as you . . . he'd tell them every one exactly what to do.

III

Further Cuttings with Endeavors
& Repeated Incantation

1 Humea Elegans

Desirable for fragrance. Straight from New South Wales.
The Lady Hume had several from those seeds communicated
by Sir Joseph Banks. Wormleybury, Herts.
Partakes in panicle the odour of the Hautboy, flowers
by July. The stem herbaceous, round, and filled
with spongy pith, pubescence.
Leaves are sessile, lanceolate, acute, and slightly
waved about the edge. Receptacle is small and glandular,
all destitute of scales. Florets fertile, regular.
Oblong germen cloven style and stigmas spreading,
capitate. Seed without a crown without a wing.

   *

Place it in the old Linnaean book beside the *Eupatorium*.
Genus undetermined until summer of '04.
Calyx loosely imbricated. Antheras is awned.

Endeavors

Goethe was impressed: he found the
plates he gazed at more exacting than
his old florilegium. These German Bauers
working off in England aimed at more
than pleasing royal patrons with the bright
and beautiful—they'd draw with great affection
even ugly weeds: also palmates & the white
clusters tinged with red and brown of an
Aesculus hippocastanum—Stubby tree he'd
drawn himself whose flower he had
pressed between the pages of a *Faust*,
whose two spiked pods he'd left in sunlight
at the corner of his botanizing desk.
The grading of these tones. These discs & cones.
This book in which all nature was made visible
and art was all concealed . . .

His drawing, he would tell you, was today
more efficacious than his word. Still, he'd
premise his endeavors under headings
stem and *leaf* and *flower* and set you straight
about your task & his:—However short, there's
always some degree of curve in stems, and
therefore you must never use a rule; practice
at your stroke and learn to draw the parallels;
then mark off the springs of every lamina.
Blades are more or less erect and you must
draw the opposites a bit awry, and if
the stem is branched then certain leaves of course
must be foreshortened. In digitates you indicate
the petiole and midribs first to orient with
greater certainty the relative anatomies;
teeth of calyx always point between divisions
of corolla. Discriminate between a keel & wing.
And to avoid the common error perpetrated
on the flower making it put on a comic air
by twisting it upon its stalk, observe with

fierce exactitude and cultivate an equanimity.
There is no other cluster like the one you've pressed
into your book. Seed pods open.
Chestnuts. Dark eyes & a Mephistophelian look.

2 Rhododendron Arboreum

Flowers late in May or early June, provincial
name is *Boorans*. The stem is columnar,
twenty feet in height, more than twenty inches
in diameter. Branches are ascending, scattered,

crooked, brittle; leaves at summits on their downy
footstalks all are ovate-lanceolate, acute,
all entire and revolute; smooth & shining green above,
clothed beneath with white dense downiness.

       *

Clusters terminal of
ten to fifteen large pedunculated crimson flowers
spread in all directions!

              Bracteas very small . . .

Calyx permanent, obtuse, and reddish at the edge;
Corolla with a longish bell-shaped tube
and lobes all cloven, rounded.

Stamens, ten: declining, smooth, inserted in receptacle.
Antheras incumbent, germen white,
seeds ovate compressed and smooth and brown

and brought to our attention thanks to Captain Hardwich
from a tour in Hindoostan—
85 degrees east longitude in the Sewalic chain.

Endeavors

And Jean-Jacques Rousseau had thrown a turnip
in the face of David Hume. It made him
feel at peace, just the way that he had felt before
the Calvinists expelled him from Geneva.

Happiness had been beyond the instigators
of a lapidation that had sent him first with
gilded papers to enfold each grass and moss
and lichen on the Island of St. Peters, then
with Hume and Boswell on to Staffordshire
as refugee where there among the rocks
and sheep and rabbits he complained that he
could find no trace of scordium and had been
stoned by Hume's appalling outcry in his sleep
when they had shared a room in Roye:
Je tiens Jean-Jacques Rousseau!

Lapwings from Laputa swarmed upon him
in the Wooton fields, the meadows of Dove Dale.
The stigma was the apex of his pistil
and he'd pollinate unless he drew a breath
into his spiracle, unless he saw the eyespot there
among the algae. Insect. Eyesore. Everyone
should march along a stipule who couldn't
stipulate for any decent stipend for philosophy!
He waited for stigmata to appear. He purged
himself with tamarinds and senna, jalop
and a dash of scammony. He'd make their
lapidation lapidary, cast his own heraldic stone,
mix the henbane in the English herbal's ink.

The turnip was enough. . . . Relieved, insane,
endeavoring to float at peace upon his prose
as once he floated on his back across the waters
of St. Peter's lake, he wrote epistles to his
cousin & her daughter. *When the rays of spring
reveal in your garden hyacinths & tulips,*

jonquils & the lilies-of-the-valley, notice that the
cabbages and cole-feed, radishes and turnips
also will appear. . . .
When you find them double,
do not meddle with them for they are deformed;
nature cannot any longer live among the monsters and
the mutilated, cannot say as she was wont to say
even in the days of lapidation

Je tiens Jean-Jacques Rousseau!

3 *Mirabilis Longiflora*

There is no colored figure of this long-flowered
Marvel of Peru: Linnaeus notes that
pollen of this plant is very large and globular and
very yellow too and hanging by a little thread
and neither falling off or bursting. . . .

The corolla presses it to stigma while the papillae
attach themselves to particles of
pollen and imbibe. . . .
                                    If raised on a hotbed like
a tender kind of annual, it blooms
in the autumn in a copious succession of rare flowers . . .

sessile at the top of every branch
and downy and extremely viscid of exterior.

      *

Seeds procured by some astronomers who knew
the celebrated M. le Monnier? Hence to Baron Munchausen
and Stockholm and to Miller's Chelsea garden and a note
in both the *Dictionary* and *Transactions*.

Stem is four feet high & forked, spreading, round & downy.
Limb is white and plaited with its five
external folds and an orifice of stunning royal purple.

Stigma large and globular and with a tuft of hairs.

Stamens are like long and silky threads.
One large tessellated nut
that's farinaceous and succeeds each flower.

Endeavors

Munificence! said Dr. Robert Thornton, bowing at
the Russian's happy approbation of his work.
Alexander, Emperor and Tzar, had smiled on La Majestieuse
engraved at great expense from a painting made for
Flora's very Temple, Thornton's book, illustrated by the
author's tables and dissections, but also by the plates
that pandered to a rage for Picturesque: like Thornton's prose,
the page *majestically presented finely-polished
bosoms to enquiring eyes.*

Utile and *Dulce*, he'd insisted on them both.
Or *Dulce* first, then *Utile*. In some proportion anyway,
and no generic backgrounds for the men
to whom the likes of Mrs. Siddons sat, who was no more
than Dr. Johnson competition for a Nodding Renealmia
or Pontic Rhododendron: *no avenues of upright timber,
gravel walks that meet by some small pond or
commonplace cascade, but scenery appropriate indeed
appropriated, brought up with the roots—*

The serious roots, e.g., of Night-blowing Cereus:
Moonlight Pether's moon was told to play
on dimpled water and the Gothic turret clock *to point
at twelve, midnight hour that finds this candle
light of orange petals at its full expanse;*
Of Mimosa Grandiflora too: and Mr. Reinagle
was asked to paint *two humming birds from
mountains in Jamaica & an aborigine who waxes all
astonished at their stationary hovering all over & about.*

Dodecatheon in the Warner aquatint was blown like
Yankee Cowslip in a *gentle breeze* required also
*to fill out the sails of a ship that flies the ensign
of our former colonies and waft around the specimen
indigenous and delicate bright butterflies.*
Too much of something here. Or maybe not enough.
At any rate, the public did not buy. Back in Moscow

his Munificence was busy with Napoleon at the very
moment when the project needed something of a boost.

The tulips named for Earl Spencer and a duchess who
had promised patronage suddenly looked dour
and frankly parsimonious beside the open petals of
Le Roy, La Majestieuse, and La Triomphe Royale
in Earlem's greatest mezzotint. Thornton raged against
infuriate war which like devouring conflagration feasts
on commerce, agriculture and the arts, the sanguine theatre
in which the armed diffuse all rapine fire & murder and
because of which the rich are taxed beyond philanthropy.

He gazed on purple Dragon Arum and he wrote:
This foetid poisonous plant! She comes all peeping
from her purple crest with mischief fraught.
A noisome vapour issues from her nostrils and infects
the ambient air; her hundred arms are interspersed
with white as in the garments of the inquisition.
From her covert there projects a spear of darkest jet;
her sex is strangely intermingled with the opposite.
Confusion dire! Her friend is Maggot-bearing Stapelia.

I am undone by what my eyes & hands have wrought!

4 Cyamus Nelumbo

Native of the silent pools, recesses, and margins
of the running streams. Will take root in deep
and muddy soil. *Tamara* or *Lotus* or *Nelumbo* :—
see the sacred poetry of Hindus. Many prohibitions
from Pythagoras to the Egyptian priests.

Root is large & tuberous, black without & white within,
growing fibres numerous & long. Leaves are radical
on long and round and prickly upright stalks;
peltate, circular, and waved; rather glaucous
and with many radiating ribs.
Young, they float upon the quiet water.
Flowers on the simple naked stalks like those of leaves,
but taller, solitary, upright, fragrant, fine.

                    *

Calyx, four or five green concave ovate leaves.
Many petals, ovate & acute, a pale rose and marked
with many crimson ribs which, drawn together as they reach
the point, deepen in their hue. Many stamens, yellow
knobbed with oblong anthers. Germen green and smooth
and conical, its upper surface perforated with the holes
that open into many cells. Every cell contains the rudiment
of seed, protruding through the orifice & crowned
with oblong and obtuse and perforated yellow stigma.

                    *

All of this becomes a coriaceous capsule, breaks off
from the stalk all laden with its oval nuts, and floats on
down the water as a cornucopia of sprouting plants.
As all Pythagorean prohibitions now are obsolete,
perhaps these beans, imported from East Indies, may
one day be welcome on our tables as a wholesome dish.

Made to flower in the Duke of Portland's stove.

Endeavors

Although apocrypha would plant his pizzle
in the garden like a tulip bulb, the truth is that
the flower Bonaparte was known to favor
was the violet. There on Elba. Even on St. Helena.
And to the utter consternation of the English.
While the amputated bulb of his virility blossomed
in a thousand tales, the violet, much relieved,
returned to little hamlets and the village greens
in England. Sedition was no longer toasted in
the name of Corporal V or conspiracy acknowledged
Elle reparaîtra au Printemps. March violet, dog violet,
yellow violet, heart's ease: *And there is pansies,
that's for thoughts.* Who'd go a-mothering and find
the violets in the lane? Who'd strew a path to the altar,
mark a page in the book? Beyond the sickbed swelled
the purple fields. Lovers would lie down in them
and slowly braid their amulets and charms.

In 1821, the final year when Bonaparte could hope
to reappear *au Printemps*, Goethe published his objections
to the "loose concupiscence" and "constant orgies"
of the stamens & the pistils taking place among Linnaeans
who refused to propagate by morphogenesis,
and violets bloomed on every bank. Among the snow drops,
primroses, arum & anemones that marked the spring,
not a single violet grew Napoleonic;
they spread all over England as they always had.
They spread through the counties, spread through
the years, Diana raising them from Io's body
for the Father of the Gods—& also for the Slade Professor
John Ruskin who went out into his Brantwood garden
looking for a specimen in 1881.
The clump he pulled out with an angry fist
reminded him of Effie's pubic hair.

Which had annoyed him like all the prurient obscenities
that Goethe had attacked in the Linnaeans.
He wouldn't draw these flowers even for his book.

He'd rather have old Bony back.
He'd rather have his wife's pudenda smooth as petals
on a Canna Lily, hairless as a billiard ball.
He'd have her like the nine year old Miss Rose La Touche.
He wrote in *Proserpina* that *disorderly & lanky, stiff
and springless stalks were bent in crabbed & broken
ways like spikes run up from some iron-foundry
for a vulgar railway station or like angular & dog-eared
gaspipes with their ill-hemmed leaves.*
He'd have it out, he'd be entirely rid of it.
No one in the world could want to draw this clump
of flowers, *mixed together, crumpled,
hacked about as if some cow had chewed on them
and left them tough and bitter, bad.*

And she had left him years before, the marriage
quietly annulled by reason of their failure to consummate.
And Rose La Touche had died quite mad.
He was relieved, he was distraught.
He had endeavored to instruct his wife about—
it did not matter, for she would not learn.
Now he'd teach the English nation how to draw their flowers,
the English workingmen about the *Fors Clavigera*.
But there was Effie in Millais' *The Order of Release*
where every stranger in the gallery could see.
He felt imprisoned still. His stamen never
touched her pistil once. He held it in his hand
among the violets & felt like Bonaparte at Austerlitz.
Elle reparaîtra au Printemps!

5 *Ipomopsis Elegans*

Dillenius said Catesby found this plant
a hundred miles from Charlestown in South Carolina.
It grows in sandy places, flowering in June.
Very difficult of cultivation for we found that
only one in twenty Catesby seeds have vegetated.

A fine drawing by the late and friendly gifted sister
of our good acquaintance Mr. Lee is in the hands
we understand of the Marquis of Blandford.
We have also seen an imitation cut in coloured paper
in possession of the Lady Banks.

       *

Much uncertainty about the genus. The learned Jussieu
supposed it might be readily reduced to his *Cantua*;
but Michaux in regarding it as something new because of
membranes in the calyx is correct. And so we take his name
which will express this flower's dazzling brilliancy.

       *

Stem is straight and wand-like to the height of several feet
where it is panicled. Leaves pinnatifid with long
and narrow segments; radicals the shortest and the broadest.

Flowers terminal and lateral appearing on short stalks
and drooping down. Calyx bell-shaped, cut above half-way
in awl-like equal parts; corolla thrice the length and

funnel-shaped, its border cleft in five and brilliant red,
Stamens springing from the upper part of tube.
Antheras is round and yellow, germen ovate smooth obtuse

and pale green. Style red and thread-like, length about the
same as stamens, with a red & three-cleft spreading stigma.
Seeds are several in each cell, acutely angular, not winged.

Endeavors

To map, to classify. And that these two endeavors
are the same. Or similar. And to collect.
A kind of madness or a kindness of the sane.
And then to draw and paint what has been
mapped and classified. Why not.
And to admire that. Or not. And pay for it,
or even make it pay. Where two such endeavors are
the same, is Shelley's Lady ever present there.

In the garden there are many houses. Shall
the husbands leave them and take ship, and shall
the wives become dependent on the bees. For there
are eunuch houses where the anthers have departed
and the stamens walk a pitching deck like Captain Cook.
In what far sea. And in what key to shanty
their polygamous designs. A few hermaphrodites
were left behind when John Paxton read into the night

at Chatsworth gardens to his duke. It was a poem
in which a garden dies because some kind
of grace has been withdrawn. The Duke of Devonshire
himself was called Your Grace and thought his great
Conservatory very heaven. He'd sent his agent off
to Chirrapoonje in the Khasi hills to bring him
Amherstia nobilis for his house of glass. And he had
brought her there. He'd classified and mapped.

He'd found his way by water to Chhatak, down
the Surma River where entire trees were covered in the
epiphytes all listed in the EIC's Calcutta book, and
he had nursed, like Buddha's monks at monasteries,
tribute of a blood-red flower paid by Chirrapoonje
in the Khasi hills to Chatsworth garden and its duke
who gazed upon it while his gardener read,
sitting by his side, & while a gaudy garden died.

A Lady—the wonder of her kind, whose form was upborn
by a lovely mind, tended the garden in the poem he read.
She did not map or classify. She sprinkled water from a stream.
The duke had sent his husbands pitching on a deck.
They sang their shanties in an unknown key. The wives
became dependent on the bees while Paxton read his Shelley.
The epiphytes were listed in the book the EIC had nursed.
The duke's *Amherstia* had been acknowledged as the first

to grow in England. Never mind. Or mind. Who'd classify
and map. Who'd say that two endeavors were the same.
Who'd read aloud while Chirrapoonje drowned and grace
collected in monsoons above the Khasi hills where no one
painted and where no one drew. The duke had drawn
his household to his side to watch him sitting by his flower
while Paxton read from Shelley's poem and epiphytes grew
up Calcutta trees. The Lady sprinkled water on hermaphrodites

and spoke of no polygamous designs. The duke had asked
John Paxton for this poem. He'd sent his agent off to
Chirrapoonje in the Khasi hills; bee and mayfly kissed
the sweet lips of his flower where sanity is madness
of the kind. O Kin, the Lady was without companions
of the mortal race and yet it was as if some spirit had deserted
paradise and lingered with her there, a veil of daylight quite
concealing it from her. Or him, the duke. Who cares.

The gardener who read the poem. But no one off in
Chirrapoonje in the Khasi hills where stamens braced against
monsoons and anthers broke off in the storm. The nullas filled;
the pools flowed; the Brahmaputra delta and the Surma ran
with smallpox, ague, dysentery. Incense burned in temples
and the dung fires in wattle huts among the palms.
The crystal shattered, crystal shatters here.
The monsoon struck. Shards of glass flew everywhere

as Paxton read. Roses, figs, convolvulus had lined the banks.
The insects bred malaria. The sound of waterfalls had drowned
the cries of birds. Or not. The birdsong was so loud
it drowned the roar of waterfalls and broken glass. The Lady

listened, stopped. Rain poured through the broken roof
in torrents and the loathliest of weeds began to grow. No need
to water there where thistles, nettles, henbane, hemlock
choked the great conservatory with malignant undergrowth.

No need to map or classify or call dissimilar endeavors
much the same. No reason to collect or draw
or paint or pay for anything or try to make it pay.
A kind of madness is the kindness of the sane if only off
across the jheels you run toward Poonji like the Dawk
become a living duke. A duck perhaps. In Devonshire.
Or there in Chirrapoonje in the Khasi hills.
The Lady stared at Paxton and the poem of Shelley fills

the page with weeds. Fungi, mildew, mold began to grow
upon His Grace's cheek; a moss upon his thigh.
And hour by hour once the air was still, the vapors rose
which have the strength to kill. The baboos in Calcutta
planted seeds to cultivate the English peach and plum.
The gardener had ceased to read. The Lady now could
only plead, there in the shattered crystal house, for more.
But all was silent as it had been long before.

5 Homo sapiens

Once beyond the troglodyte, the tailed man, the satyr.
Once beyond the pygmy among anthropoids. . .
Homo monstrosus: the giants and the dwarfs.
Once beyond the *homo monstrosus* the *homo sapiens*.

*

Some are fair and sanguine, brawny, and with
yellow flowing hair. Eyes blue & gentle & acute.
These are covered closely in their vestments;
These are always governed by their laws.

Others copper-colored and choleric.
Hair is black & straight & thick; the harsh face,
the scanty beard. These are obstinate, content, & free.
These are regulated by their customs.

*

Others sooty, melancholy, rigid.
Eyes dark; severe and haughty, covetous.
These are covered always in loose garments.
These are governed by opinions.

Still others black & blacker & phlegmatic;
frizzled hair, the flat nose, the tumid lips.
These are indolent and negligent.
These are only governed by caprice.

*

Baptize as we do the sea routes and the landmarks.
Baptize as we do the flowers.
Know thyself as European Sapiens.
Strut the Latin long Linnaean names.

sail archangel agrimony avens
broom & burdock

eyebright fumitory meadow sweet
so the mountain flax & mugwort so the sanicle

and all indigenous medicinals be meet

elsewhere also sail & what's the use
& where's the hemlock woodsage yarrow find

some bird of paradise

& what's archangel agrimony avens to
strelitzia reginae

la triomphe royale la majestieuse

cuttings & endeavors & a mezzotint
record a bank & there the wild thyme blows

& oxlips & the nodding violet grows

Sources

Much of this sequence draws directly, without external attribution, from a wide range of poems, letters, journals, and scientific literatures of the 18th and early 19th centuries, as well as from contemporary scholarly and critical sources. The "cuttings" have been made, mostly, from the following works.

Part I

Lyric epigraph: Edith Grey Wheelwright, *Medicinal Plants and Their History;* William Shakespeare, *A Midsummer Night's Dream.*

Sections numbered 1–5, "John Tradescant" to "Richard Spruce": Kenneth Lemmon, *The Golden Age of Plant Hunters;* Charles Lyte: *The Plant Hunters;* M. Hadfield, *Pioneers in Gardening;* S. Parkinson, *A Journal of a Voyage to the South Seas;* Kingdom F. Ward, *The Romance of Plant Hunting.*

"Endeavors" 1–5: J. C. Beaglehole, ed., *The Endeavour Journal of Joseph Banks;* Patrick O' Brien, *Joseph Banks;* John Gascoigne, *Joseph Banks and the English Enlightenment: Useful Knowledge and Polite Culture;* Ronald King, *Royal Kew;* Richard Mabey, *The Flowers of Kew;* Robert Hughes, *The Fatal Shore;* K. A. Austin, *The Voyage of the Investigator.*

Part II

"As Kew As You": Ronald King, *Royal Kew;* Richard Mabey, *The Flowers of Kew;* The Rev. W. Mason, "Heroic Epistle to Sir William Chambers"; Erasmus Darwin, "Botanic Garden"; Stephen Duck, "The Thresher's Labour"; Thomas Chatterton, "Kew Gardens"; Fanny Burney, the Diaries and the Letters; Wilfrid Blunt, *The Art of Botanical Illustration;* Gordon Dunthorne, *Flower and Fruit Prints of the 18th and Early 19th Centuries.*

Part III

Sections numbered 1–5, "Humea Elegans" to "Ipomopsis Elegans": James Edward Smith, *Exotic Botany: Consisting of Coloured Figures and Scientific Descriptions of such New, Beautiful, or Rare Plants as are Worthy of Cultivation in the Gardens of Britain; with Remarks on their Qualities, History, and Requisite Modes of Treatment.*

"Endeavors" 1–5: Wilfrid Blunt, *The Art of Botanical Illustration;* Jean-Jacques Rousseau, *Letters on the Elements of Botany Addressed to a Lady;* C. E. Vulliamy,

Rousseau; William H. Blanchard, *Rousseau and the Spirit of Revolt;* Robert John Thornton, *The Temple of Flora;* Hugh Macmillan, *The Poetry of Plants;* John Ruskin, *Proserpina;* John Dixon Hunt, *The Wider Sea: A Life of John Ruskin;* Alan Bewell, *Jacobin Plants: Botany as Social Theory in the 1790s;* Mary Louise Pratt, *Imprial Eyes: Travel Writing and Transculturation;* Judith Pascoe, *Female Botanists and the Poetry of Charlotte Smith;* Kenneth Lemmon, *The Golden Age of Plant Hunters;* Percy Bysshe Shelley, "The Sensitive Plant."

"Homo Sapiens": Linnaeus, as quoted in Edward Dudley and Maximillian E. Novak, eds., *The Wild Man Within;* Michel Foucault, *The Order of Things.*